What Boundaries? Live Your Dream!

Two Women. Twelve Countries. One enormous backpack and a dream to see the world!

Lisa Chavis
&
Cheryl MacDonald

Wander Press
Lithia, Florida USA
www.WanderPress.com

What Boundaries? Live Your Dream!
Two women. Twelve countries. One enormous backpack and a dream to see the world!

by Lisa Chavis and Cheryl MacDonald

Copyright © 2010 by Lisa Chavis & Cheryl MacDonald
Cover Photos © 2010 by Lisa Chavis & Cheryl MacDonald

Published by **Wander Press**
16765 FishHawk Blvd. #319
Lithia, FL 33547 USA
www.WanderPress.com

All rights reserved. No part of this book may be reproduced or transmitted in any form without written permission from the publisher, except by reviewers who may quote brief excerpts in connection with a review.

Library of Congress Control Number: 2009936601

ISBN-10: 0-9841320-0-7
ISBN-13: 978-0-9841320-0-3

First Edition

Dedication

For All Those Who Dream...

Dedication

Acknowledgements

A trip like this is truly a dream come true, but it couldn't have happened without help from so many people.

THANK YOU!!!

To **Sandy, Steve,** and **Ryan** for providing us a home during our travels. Sharing your home, garage, and laundry with two homeless travelers is something we'll never forget.

To **Jamie** and **Teresa** for taking care of the mail the entire trip and saving us by sending a new driver's license and credit cards when we were pick-pocketed in Paris.

To **Paula** and **Thom** for giving a loving home to Woobie and Bugzi. Never have two kitties been so spoiled!

To **Sue** and **Jim** for providing support and understanding when your forty year old daughter nervously told you she was going to quit her job, sell everything, and travel the world. Your response of "What took you so long?" sealed the deal.

To **Sandy** and **Deidre** for pouring tequila shots at a six AM garage sale.

To **Beth Whitman** for giving us a voice and our first blog on her website Wanderlustandlipstick.com.

Thank you to our hosts and hostesses along the way who shared their stories as well as their hospitality. To those friends we met in hostels who taught us the correct way to label food in a communal kitchen and told us of places not to miss along the way.

Also to the German tourists in the Nice airport, "So sorry for trapping you on the moving walkway! I hope you made your flight."

The Journey

Introduction		9
Chapter 1	Luggage	11
Chapter 2	Beginnings	19
Chapter 3	Ireland	25
Chapter 4	Dublin * Kilkenny * Killarney	31
Chapter 5	Brussels, Belgium	45
Chapter 6	Paris, France	53
Chapter 7	Mont St. Michel * Blois, France	63
Chapter 8	Lyon and Marseille * Nice, France	75
Chapter 9	Grosseto * Viterbo, Italy	83
Chapter 10	Civitavecchia, Rome * Catania, Sicily * Izmir, Turkey * Patmos * Mykonos * Santorini, Greece	93
Chapter 11	Rome, Italy	105
Chapter 12	Florence * Greve in Chianti * Vinci, Italy	113
Chapter 13	Venice * Susa, Italy	121
Chapter 14	Bayonne * Biarritz, France * Madrid, Spain	135
Chapter 15	Valencia * Barcelona, Spain	145
Chapter 16	Vouvery * Zweisimmen * Gstaad, Switzerland * Vaduz, Liechtenstein * St. Anton, Austria	153
Chapter 17	Bad Gastein * Freistadt, Austria * Prague, Czech Republic	165
Chapter 18	Regensburg * Munich, Germany	177
Chapter 19	Epernay * Paris, France	185
Chapter 20	Paris, France * Tampa, Florida USA	191
About the Travelers		195
Questions and Answers		197

Introduction

The purpose of the book you hold in your hands is twofold. First, it's the story of a journey and the life lessons learned. Second, it's an attempt to awaken that spirit of adventure lying deep, cozy, and dormant in us all. But beware! Once the mischievous sprite wakes up, there is no limit to what breathtaking, surprising, and extraordinary events await.

There are moments in your life when you realize things will NEVER be same. Giving up the lives we knew to step out and live a dream of traveling around the world was one of those times. In so many ways it felt like the moment our lives really began. This book is about the beginning of that journey. We chose to visit twelve countries in thirteen weeks, not to simply put a pin on the map, but to find a true feeling of place and people.

While we traveled, our focus changed from us as individuals to the part we play in this enormous world-wide community. We were astounded at how motivating and inspiring this kinship became. The bonds of friendship we made (and continue to make) along the way shaped our adventure and lent a priceless personal aspect to the fun. With that in mind, this book is being promoted almost entirely through Internet social media. Before we began to travel, we didn't realize the power of keeping in contact through such applications like Facebook or Twitter. In fact, these weren't even in our vocabulary!

Today it's a new world and one in which we hope to share our smiles and adventures with a goal of encouraging others to look for the courage and motivation to live their own dream! Come laugh along with us…

"Life is either a daring adventure or nothing" **– Helen Keller**

There were a thousand reasons why we shouldn't do this, but those eight words were enough to convince us that we should.

Cheryl & Lisa

I

"He who would travel happily must travel light."

- - St. Exuprey

Luggage

There are few chunky backpackers.

I made this astute observation while packing for our trip through Europe. Granted, the adventure magazines always show the most beautiful human specimens alongside this year's top-of-the-line gear. I can't say I blame them. If I were Kelty or Osprey and I'd spent lots of money developing the bag capable of holding it all, it would be a great disappointment to see it strapped to the back of someone who looked like me. Now, I wouldn't say I'm morbidly obese or anything close – but I am carrying a few too many Big Macs around my middle. I don't look anything at all like those svelte backpacker models with hard abs and calves chiseled from stone. Looking in the mirror it's hard to tell what's lumpier, the backpack or me.

But backpacking was a sport anyone could do, right? Toss a few things in a pack; pick it up, put the whole thing in the RV, and you're off for a great camping trip. Easy enough.

"What exactly goes in a backpack, anyway?" I asked, trying to read the upside down checklist from the camping magazine my friend Cheryl was reading. Cheryl is the planner for this journey. She draws up the lists and as my traveling companion her job is as important as ensuring we have a corkscrew onboard. You see, I have extreme list phobia.

"The usual stuff. Food – that freeze-dried kind. A flint. Some matches. A sleeping bag. Don't worry. I'll make a list."

"Um. About this backpacking thing. I thought we'd be living in a little more civilized way." My imagination ran more in the direction of seaside evening dining on the French Riviera or sipping fine wine from a balcony in Tuscany. Were we really planning on eating freeze-dried food? Eww. And what would we do with a flint? "I'm not so sure I'm okay with this."

"We're going to be on a budget traveling all over Europe and we have to be ready for anything. It will be better to have something we don't need than to need something we don't have." This prophetic statement spelled H-E-A-V-Y in my mind, but I agreed.

We'd start with the backpack.

So began our sporting goods store visits, one after another, faithfully trying on, snapping clips, snugging buckles, hoisting to our shoulders for a quick romp around the aisles, dodging exercise machines and enduring the eye-watering new rubber smell of bicycle tires.

Once we had the list narrowed down to those with the best fit, specifically made for a woman's torso, with a pocket for a water bladder (important to carry your water low on your back, the Gear Guide said), and were the right color – this was very important! I wanted red, Cheryl wanted blue – now we were ready to complete our purchases.

Cheryl hit the Internet to find the best deals. Soon she had negotiated free shipping and next day delivery. I called from work to see if the package had arrived. I was so excited. Looking back, I now wonder what on earth I was thinking.

It looked easy in the magazines. Never mind that the closest I'd ever come to carrying a rucksack (what the "real" travelers call a backpack) for any distance was between classes during my college years. A long time ago. I lived on-campus, so the only things I carried were a notebook, a pen, and a super-sized bag of peanut M&Ms for energy.

In the sporting goods store, the pack I selected seemed fine. Three pounds felt a tad on the heavy side, but I was sure I could adapt. After all, I was going to "backpack across Europe". It sounded completely cool and adventurous.

"Wow! You're backpacking through Europe? Amazing!" Looks of pure envy came my way each time I used those words.

In the weeks before the trip, I started to begin every conversation with, "Yes, I'm backpacking across Europe for thirteen weeks." Likely, some of those looks I perceived as envy were carefully concealed thoughts of: *Is she out of her mind? Is this a mid-life crisis? She's not as young or fit as those kids in the backpacker magazines. How will she manage?*

Still, in my mind, I was trekking through the mountains of Austria – the Von Trappe family as my guide. In my vision, my lederhosen fit snug as a glove and the pack sat weightless on my shoulders because I'd done the research and found the perfect fit.

The backpacks arrived! We reverently unpacked them, staring in awe at the pretty colors. Special cords and loops were there to hold all manner of things. I wasn't sure what they were meant to hold (maybe an ice axe and M&M's?), but I was positive it would be useful to have them, just in case.

"I can see us now," I mused, "summiting Mt. Kilimanjaro in the crystal clear dawn to the applause and accolades of two hundred of our closest friends. It will be a moment we'll never forget."

"Lisa, we're going to Europe. Not Africa. There will be no cameras from National Geographic following us," Cheryl explained.

I sighed. So my geography was a bit off – as it proved to be more than once on this European journey. A tiny taste of what was in store for us along the way.

Cheryl came up with a great idea. "Let's fill the packs with towels for bulk and put in a ten pound weight. If we carry them around everywhere for the next few weeks, we'll be ready when it comes time for the trip." She's so smart! I ran off to get my towels and my ten pounds.

Holy cow! This is heavy!, I thought to myself as I hoisted the pack.

"This feels great," Cheryl chirped as she practically ran around the room with her loaded pack. "I think carrying these will be a breeze."

I didn't dare share my concerns to Cheryl. This was only ten pounds and a few towels. We estimated my pack would hold twenty-five pounds and Cheryl's thirty-five. Maybe I'd got the wrong pack in the mail. This one, even empty, felt much heavier than it had in the store a week ago.

We planned to go on a "prep hike" with the packs. Fill them up with fun stuff – a bottle of wine and a bucket of fried chicken – head out to a popular park, hike out as far as we were able to walk and come back. This would get us ready for the road.

I used up every justification in my well-worn excuse book. "It's too hot," "the bugs are really bad today", "it's going to rain and we'll get soaked"; until we ran out of time and our best laid plans to prepare for carrying the packs around Europe were just a memory.

It was getting close now. Most of the trip purchases had been bought and stowed. Lists checked and re-checked. Everything was a go and it was time for a dry run.

Having recently become homeless after selling all our worldly possessions, Cheryl and I were staying with friends who were kind enough to let us store our "trip stuff" in their garage. A beautiful Saturday morning held all the promise of the new adventure awaiting us.

We pulled out everything we'd need for the thirteen weeks, sorted and checked it off the list. Shoes…socks…underwear…shirts… Somewhere after shirts and way before pants, I ran out of room in my pack. I shoved, scrunched, and stomped on the sack in a vain attempt to get more inside. It wasn't happening. All the secret pockets were stuffed until the zippers strained. And I was still looking at a big pile of stuff that absolutely had to go. I was close to panic. I'd pared down my belongings four times. No wiggle room remained for leaving anything out at this point.

"This thing should hold enough for four people," I muttered. Zippers, uncovering secret pouches, were now straining under willful socks and panties. The backpack was so deceptive. It looked huge – 3500 cubic inches, the tag read. This bag was the opposite of those tiny cars capable of holding hold one hundred clowns. This one looked as though it could hold all my stuff and the neighbors with plenty of room to spare. In reality, however, it was full after only a few items. Shaking my head in despair, I went back to The Guide for help.

To remedy the space issue, The Guide recommended buying compression sacks and packable bags designed to squish down to nothing once the air is pushed out of them. These squishy bags were a great help on the trip early on. Put in a pile of clothes, seal it up, and roll until all the air is out. Presto – extra space. This wasn't quite as wonderful as it sounds. As we used these every day, by the middle of the trip, the seals got leaky. Often times, my backpack would suddenly swell up like a giant Puffer fish, straining the zippers until I could get back in and re-seal everything.

Cheryl graciously offered to carry some of my things, as her pack was bigger. I'd purchased the "woman-torso" model to accommodate my lack of height. The smaller size, however, drastically cut down on my available space for stuffing stuff. But Cheryl's pack was already full. She was carrying the laundry gear and we needed to be sure some room was left over, as it was sure to expand as our pile of dirty clothes grew.

My dilemma grew worse as back in the house I found even more items I deemed absolutely necessary for personal contentment on this trip. Two books and a magazine seemed insignificant until space became such a premium. Cheryl suggested a small daypack in addition to the large rucksack. This was almost the answer. Only now the daypack loaded with a laptop computer (although a small one), two cameras and their assorted charging devices was almost as heavy as the one I was carrying on my back. I'd run out of appendages to tote things. Disappointment and panic were growing exponentially as the trip drew closer.

Desperate, I went to the Internet for a solution. What did others do who had to take more stuff than their collective packs would hold?

A large duffle was one answer. Put the large rucksack and the daypack together in one duffle, sling the whole thing over one shoulder and off you'd go. Sounded as though it was a good idea to me. Off I went to the sporting goods store (again) and came back with the biggest duffle Columbia produced. It was almost longer than I was tall. Surely this one would hold everything I needed to take, right? Right! It held it all and even had room to spare. I was ecstatic. It would all fit and I wouldn't have to leave anything important behind. I proudly showed my new purchase to Cheryl; sure she'd be impressed by my ability to solve my problem with such efficiency.

Kindly, but with a slight touch of skepticism, she took a good look at the enormous black lump. "Can you lift it?"

Of course I could lift it. I hadn't tried to lift it yet, but I was sure I could. If I was able to carry each of the packs individually, together they shouldn't be a problem.

Uh-huh. My God, it was heavy. And incredibly unwieldy. One pack shifted in one direction, while the other wrapped around my legs as I staggered a few steps toward the door. But I was determined. "I'll be able to do it," I said with a confidence borne of desperation.

"Well, you can always give it a try in Seattle and if it works, take the duffle to Europe. But you don't look comfortable."

I shot her a glaring look, my face already beet red from trying to hoist the lumbering duffle onto my shoulder and stagger to the door, the bag a mere two inches from the floor.

We'd planned a vacation in Seattle with a friend well before the idea for the European adventure took hold, now this would be an opportunity to test out the solution to my packing woes.

"I've got it. I'll be fine. Just quit looking at me," I muttered. As soon as I was safely outside the door, I dropped the sack and wondered what I had been thinking. This wasn't much fun at all.

As I'm sure you've figured out, Seattle was a bust as far as my luggage situation was concerned. By the time I got the giant albatross to the baggage check-in in Tampa, I was sweating profusely and swearing I'd never pack anything more than would fit in a carry-on bag, no matter how long I would be staying. When I pulled it off of the baggage claim carrousel in Seattle, I hated it. My shoulder pulled out of its socket with an audible pop and I could barely drag the awful thing across the airport floor.

My traveling companions had mercy on me and suggested we open the duffle, take everything out and share the load among us all. As much as I wanted to be rid of the thing, my pride wouldn't let me share the load. It was my stuff. My responsibility. But I did agree to open the duffle, pop the big rucksack on my back and hand-carry my daypack. It worked. By the time we returned to Tampa, I'd ditched the duffle. It is now a dark, hulking monster in my friend's garage, awaiting its next victim.

Now with only five days left until we were officially "on the road" for thirteen weeks, I was out of options. I cut down on my underwear allotment to three pairs, shoes to two pairs, and decided I didn't really need to read any books. Surely I'd find some place in Europe with a book I could beg or borrow. Tearfully, I put my good camera (too big) in storage and bemoaned the imagery I was already sure I'd be missing.

It was a total stroke of luck. A trick of fate? Divine guidance? The Universe at work? Whatever. I had everything I could possibly fit tightly stuffed in my pack with just two days to go until the wheels of our plane left the ground. I was trying not to think about what I'd be leaving behind. This trip was all about teaching me to let go of material things and this was my biggest test so far.

I was meeting some friends for a goodbye dinner at the mall and happened to walk by the brand new, just opened, still-smells-like-fresh-paint – Dick's Sporting Goods. I looked around the cavernous room with an awe I've only previously experienced in the Notre Dame Cathedral. It was as if the enormous tent set up in the middle of the store was put there just as a beacon for me. Drawing me closer. Deep into the camping department. Closer. Until I saw it. It was what I had been destined to find. A super-sized, larger-than-life, gynormous RED backpack. Red, my favorite color. It was a sign.

I picked it up and peered inside, my voice echoing through the deep spaces. My vow to downsize was forgotten instantly. There were huge spaces inside. So much room. Now I could bring everything I wanted and I'd still have room to spare. And did I mention it was red?

The bag wasn't specially fitted for a woman's torso. It was meant for someone six foot two inches tall with a lot of crap to carry. I didn't care. I'd manage to carry it. Somehow.

2

"Life is either a daring adventure, or nothing."

- Helen Keller

Beginnings

It started innocently enough. A question batted around the room. Three close friends and a bottle of wine. At the beginning there were three of us. Three women, all friends for more years than we could remember. Each of us standing at a time in our lives when we knew big changes were on the horizon. Words were finally in the air we hadn't dared speak out loud before this evening. Divorce, stopping work mid-career, a recent break-up – all personal events we couldn't ignore. Our lives were at a point of change.

"What would you do if you had no boundaries?" There it was. The question on the table.

"What if there were no boundaries of a mortgage or job, no full-time responsibility for children, spouse, parents or pets – absolutely nothing to hold you back?" Cheryl added.

I had to put my two cents in as well, "Or, what would you most regret *not* doing?"

Another bottle of wine was opened and the questions continued, "What if, you could do anything you wanted, go anywhere, see anything? What would you do? Where would you go? No boundaries. No limits."

Each of us took a few seconds to consider, and fired off the first thing coming to mind.

"I'd want to see places I've only dreamed of before and meet people from all walks of life. Do something to make a difference."

"I'd like to soak up local cultures and exotic foods, dive unknown waters, run along high cliffs with spectacular views and climb steps worn slick by history."

"My dream," I threw in excitedly, "is to write a book and share the world I see with someone like me who has only experienced real travel through books. Bring the world to them. Show someone if I can do it, so can they!"

We had all the answers. Now all we had to do was decide if we'd let this fantasy die or if we could throw all caution to the wind and say *Why Not?* We got together again a week later and this time the energy in the room was supercharged. We didn't even need the wine!

"Boundaries? What Boundaries? Anything can be worked around. Let's do this. Let's travel around the world. It will be an once-in-a-lifetime journey we'll never forget," our adventure-racing, ultra marathon-running friend chimed in. Somehow, in the span of one week, our thought processes had moved from *What If?* to *How?*

The innocuous travel bug had bitten and I wasn't even aware of it. Symptoms started slowly. A short detour to the bookstore to pick up yet another guidebook, the just-for-a-second look at a travel website touting voluntourism, wistful glances at a dusty globe in the library. Every day events began to show a tarnish I hadn't noticed before. I was almost ready to do this.

My newly built sandcastle of throwing all caution to the wind took a blow when our third party decided to put her dream on hold for a while. Wisely, she chose to stay close and work on personal concerns best handled in person and not thousands of miles away. Giving her a big hug, a promise to keep our dream alive, and our best assurances we'd meet up with her somewhere along the way almost derailed us.

"Do you still want to do this? It will just be the two of us," Cheryl asked. "We're very different in our traveling styles."

"I know. You're used to traveling Five Star and I prefer Dive Bars." I rolled my eyes.

"We'll be on a budget this time, so there will be lots more Dive Bars than Five Stars. And if we get too aggravated with each other, there's always duct tape."

I laughed. "This could be a huge test of our friendship, traveling together, but I think we can do it. So long as you promise not to push me off a cliff while I pose for a picture."

"What? Me?" Cheryl's imaginary halo lit up. "Could you take just few steps back…no, a few more…perfect! Just kidding! It will be an amazing experience."

"I agree. I don't know when I've been this excited about something. Let's do it!"

So this is how a question and a bottle of wine led two ordinary women on an incredible journey. It was an unusual time in our lives. Cheryl was just on the cusp of forty with a promising career as a Senior Director at a Fortune 500 company. I was much deeper into the doldrums of the decade, but had worked hard over the years to establish myself in the profession of pharmacy. If we wanted to do this, it would be with full knowledge of what we were leaving behind.

Our plan is to cover twelve countries in thirteen weeks. And this is just the beginning of the around-the-world quest – it's all we could fit in the first book! Ireland, Belgium, France, Spain, Liechtenstein, Germany, Austria, Switzerland, Czech Republic, Turkey, Greek Isles, and Italy – nowhere is safe from our over-loaded baggage and feeble (if funny) attempts at speaking a new language at every stop.

What made the two of us ready to stand on the edge of the cliff – still deathly afraid – but willing to take that first step into the void? As with most things in life, I believe it was simply a matter of timing. There are few times when the stars line up to put people in a place where they are open to listening to their hearts and not their heads. We were at such a place.

What Boundaries? and *Why Not?* became our mantras as dreams for the trip started to coalesce into concrete reality. A For Sale sign appeared in front of the house as newly drafted letters of resignation waited anxiously on the computer. Helen Keller's words inspired as friends and neighbors carted away once prized possessions during yard sales and as pieces of our old lives disappeared into the trunks of stranger's cars. As things sold, our shared travel account at the bank grew. This was real. It was happening.

The house sold in seven days in an awful real estate market. My mother graciously offered to give my two cats a loving home until I came back. Saying goodbye to the well-worn career ladder wasn't as hard as expected. It was almost too easy.

Things started to slip a little when we realized it was too late to do anything but keep moving forward. Here's a tip. When planning your trip around the world, or any big adventure, don't start with the question, "What's the worst thing that might happen?" If your brain is anything like mine, it will take you to places you really don't need to go.

I'm a worrier by nature, so this was a lesson learned the hard way. I bolted awake at three AM, bathed in a cold sweat, heart pounding as I struggled to untangle sheets from my legs. Moments before, the sheets were giant anacondas sucking me deeper into the jungle. I'd fallen into the snake pit while running through the brush, my face covered in bug bites and scratches, cursing incoherently at the sky while holding my dead cell phone. I'm a pharmacist, not a psychiatrist, but I could already see some serious issues here.

Cheryl shared her nightmarish concerns as well. "I imagine myself sitting at a computer screen watching the falling stock markets, afraid to hit the ENTER button, while my family members watch from behind, screaming "Sell, sell, sell! Was quitting my job and giving up everything to travel the right thing to do?" Each of our innermost fears appeared almost nightly as the trip got closer – my loss of the comforts of home and Cheryl's future financial future at risk.

We were also besieged by those negative gremlins who sit on your shoulder and whisper, "How can you possibly do this?" or "What will your friends and family think?" It is not an easy thing to do, changing your life in such a huge way. Leaving a home, a career, or any safe space is a big thing. But with big conquests come even bigger rewards…or so we were hoping. Regardless of our fears and nightmares, we were also anxious to get to the adventure.

"What's that thing? A white board?" I asked as I peeked into Cheryl's office. "I've never known anyone who had such a large white board in their home before."

"It's for planning – keeping track of where, when and how we're going to get there. There's so much to plan for this trip and if it's on the board it's easier to see. We've got plane reservations, hostel reservations, dates for festivals, transportation options from country to country and a map of Europe to go over."

"Wow. Amazing. I guess I thought we'd just be taking it one day at a time." I pulled out my notebook. "Did I tell you my word for this trip is absorb? It's what I plan to do. Take in as much of the authenticity of travel as possible, write about it and absorb it." I sat down and prepared to soak up some of the hundreds of details she'd carefully printed on the board.

"You absorb, while I plan," she graciously offered.

Sounded like a great arrangement to me. Cheryl prepared all the groundwork. My job was to keep us focused on the positive. I imagined myself sitting in a Paris cafe sipping a café crème alongside Hemingway's ghost, writing quietly inspired words in my journal. Or the accolades Cheryl would receive from friends and family as she graciously accepts the Nobel Peace Prize. Or the excitement our volunteer efforts will generate to foster global and intercultural harmony through the discovery of a new shrew species in Inner Mongolia. The worries will work themselves out. For better or worse, it was time to begin a new phase of our lives.

At one of the farewell parties, Cheryl picked up our third traveler – a fuzzy, purple, stuffed octopus with the most expressive eyes I'd ever seen. We named her Priscilla.

"You have to take her along with you," a friend proposed. "She can be your mascot."

"Yes, get pictures of her at all the places you visit, we'd rather see her than you guys," another suggested. Gee, some friends we have!

So Priscilla became our constant companion. She takes up only a little space and doesn't seem to mind being stuffed into whatever backpack corner we can find. We just pull her out, fluff her up, and she's ready for her photo shoots. How many purple octopuses can say they've taken a trip around the world?

3

"The only aspect of our travels that is interesting to others is disaster."

-Martha Gellman

Ireland

The lure of rolling, green hills; black, foamy Guinness pints; and cheap airline tickets from Florida won over Ireland as the ideal launch site of our round-the-world backpacking journey. Truthfully, it could be the tidbit of trivia that each Irishman consumes an average of 131.1 liters of beer each year – the second highest quantity of beer drunk per person after the Czech Republic. And the Czech Republic isn't famous for its magical leprechauns, rainbows, or lyrical bar songs, either. This was an easy choice.

Once we settled on the country, now came the fun of selecting the places to see. Dublin, County Cork, Kilkenny, Killarney, The Ring of Kerry, the many Glens and Enns – all poetic, Irish sounding names we couldn't wait to explore. Even Muckanaghederdauhaulia, in County Galway was on the list. As the longest village name in Ireland, it means *Pig Marsh Between Two Seas*. Who wouldn't want to visit such a lovely place?

Soon "guidebook glaze" started to overtake us. Spending hours poring over a tattered guide book, studying the various maps, sights not to miss, what to do when you only have three days to see a city, where to get the best fill-in-the-blank. Whether it's the finest corned beef and cabbage, Full Irish breakfast, Irish stew, pint of Guinness (what a long list!), ancient castles, or Celtic crosses – the list grew and grew.

Our eyes turned glassy from the small printed type. We had planned to spend one week in Ireland and wanted to fill up on the sights, smells, and sounds the country had to offer. Where to start? There was so much to see and do.

It's easy to get overwhelmed with all the alternatives available – and this was just the first country of twelve we were planning to visit. So much to see, do, eat, and drink. Then there was finding places to exercise, worship, and relax. With so many choices, my overwhelmed brain shuts down.

The goal for this trip is immersing ourselves in the uniqueness of places we visit. "Black pudding? Sure, I'll have another slice." Don't ask what's in it (okay, if you really want to know, blood turns this "pudding" black. Yuck!).

But the stories to tell about these new food experiments is worth it. Cheryl is self-described as a non-adventurous eater and if I can't identify it by food group, I usually won't eat it either. This might be our biggest challenge, but we make a vow not to visit McDonalds for the entire trip.

Further guidebook reading calms any serious worries about food as we learn there are roughly 9,386 Public Houses (or Pubs) in Ireland – not counting the 1,600 in Northern Ireland, should we get hungry there. As we are suckers for good Irish pub food and a well-pulled pint, Ireland was going to be a great first choice.

Our minds became mush noting all the sites we were supposed to visit. We were overwhelmed and decided our best course was to drink several pints of Guinness rather than worrying about what Fodor's thought we should do.

Sleep was all but impossible on the Wednesday night before we left. I flipped and flopped, finally just gave up and went to pass the time on my computer. Cheryl was already out in our friend's living room, her face lit by the ghostly glow of her own laptop. She was doing what she does best; checking and re-checking the details of the trip. Looking at our stuffed backpacks waiting impatiently by the door, we whispered excitedly about the trip.

For the umpteenth time, we went over our lists, ticking off items we knew it was too late to do anything about. It soothed our nerves, enough so that when our alarms went off for real, we were ready to roll. Ready to see the world!

The ride to the airport was as lurching to my stomach as a rickety wooden rollercoaster at the fair. Only this time I couldn't just get off when the ride was over, walk over to a potted plant, and barf my previously eaten ice cream.

Morning coffee? Not for me. Cheryl would find hers at the airport Starbucks – savoring each sip, because there was no telling when we'd see another one of those again. Food? Absolutely not. My stomach tends to throw a fit whenever I fly. I didn't want to make an awful mess on the plane, as I'd have to be in these clothes for many more hours before landing in Ireland.

Once on the plane from Tampa to Newark, my worst nightmare was realized. A chatty seatmate on my left pounced as soon as I'd snapped my seatbelt closed. On a plane, I am not a talker. I prefer to bury my head in a book or magazine, keeping my arms tucked in by my side – unless they're gripping the armrest in white-knuckled panic as the plane bafflingly breaks the bonds of gravity.

I'd rather enjoy my own thoughts than those of someone else. "Are we going to fall from the sky? What was that weird noise? Did I hear something break on the engine?" My own reflections comfort me, not the small talk of a person sitting next to me.

"Where are you headed?" The Talker asked with such excitement and cheeriness it caused me to wonder what she'd slipped in her own coffee that morning.

"Newark," I mumbled and went back to reading the water evacuation procedures for the 747. I'd already positioned my barf bag within easy reach, just in case.

"Newark? Me, too," she chirped. "I'm going to a convention. I sell real estate. Do you own a house?"

I rolled my eyes and looked to Cheryl for help. She is quite the opposite of me in her plane manners. She loves to talk to people on planes. Actually, she'll talk to people everywhere. She's met some incredibly interesting people along the way. NFL quarterbacks, CEOs of companies – many she stayed in contact with through the years. I couldn't be more different. I don't like to talk to strangers on a plane. I don't like to talk to strangers anywhere.

Cheryl jumped in and immediately picked up the conversation, "Well, neither of us owns a house now. We sold almost everything – house, cars, and motorcycles, anything we couldn't fit in a backpack – to travel around the world for the next year or so."

"Oh my! You don't own a house? Where will you live when you get back? Let me give you my card." She started digging in her purse while I sat as far back in my seat as possible, sweaty palms on the seat rest, tightly shut eyes, and pretending not to notice we were straining at a nearly ninety degree angle with the ground.

Cheryl and this woman became fast friends. They spent the entire flight discussing everything from real estate to the last books they had read, over me in the middle seat, reading my magazine, and trying to ignore both of them. At least it was only a two hour flight and when we landed in Newark, I shakily stepped off the plane. It felt as though we'd really begun the journey. Onward to Ireland!

At Newark airport, we took advantage of Cheryl's airline club membership for one last time. Our plans included hostel stays throughout Ireland, so we checked and wrote e-mails, not knowing when we'd be back in touch with Wi-Fi connections. I was fighting a head cold with a barking cough and seemed to scare people whenever I got close. This could work to my advantage on our next flight.

"Are you ordering another drink?" Cheryl asked as I slurped down my third free Bloody Mary.

"Yes, want me to get you one, too?" I slid off the bar stool and tried not to topple over the man who was texting on his Blackberry next to me. "I feel a lot better. I don't know whether it's the cough syrup or the drinks, but I'm not nearly as nervous about the flight as I thought I'd be."

This was Cheryl's first time traveling to Europe and it had been many years since I'd taken the trip, so to say I was wound up is a bit of an understatement. It was hard to explain how excited I was at the little "gifts" on my seat when we boarded. Forget the typical blanket and pillow – we had our own special package of stuff for the long haul. An eye mask (in basic black), earplugs, a little lotion sample with a delightful smell, and a personal toothbrush complete with a sample of fresh, minty toothpaste. I was thrilled! Cheryl flew all the time in her previous Corporate Director position, but I was a pharmacist stuck behind a counter or a computer most of my days. She was a little mortified at how enthused I was over the presents, but once I'd convinced her to smell the lotion, she agreed it was nice.

"Doesn't this smell great?" I asked.

"Yes, it smells good," Cheryl consented.

"Yeah, but really smell this, it smells so good!"

"You're poking me in the nose, please stop it," she whispered emphatically.

"But doesn't this smell great?"

"Yes, it's wonderful. It's the nicest smelling lotion I've ever smelled. Now get it away from my nose." She buried her head in a magazine and tried to get past this lotion-smelling moment as quickly as possible.

Ours was a huge plane (more evacuation procedures to read about), two seats on a side (nobody I was forced to talk to about real estate), and all the movies we wanted to watch. Wow! We each had our own little TV screen and could look at what we wanted, when we wanted. This was going to be fun.

Flight currency in hand, I ordered my own little bottle of wine, took off my shoes, and immersed myself in Movie Land. The trip across the big ocean was uneventful, two movies, a short nap and we were making our final descent into Ireland. I could see wisps of green through the thick clouds.

One thing I hadn't thought too much about was the change in time zones we'd be going through on this trip. When we arrived in Dublin, it was just after seven in the morning. But our bodies were under the impression it was still two AM. By the time we collected our baggage and cleared customs at the airport, we desperately needed sleep. Though I believed a nice, stiff Irish coffee would be better to help ward off the feeling we were sleepwalking.

"Mine is on the second page. What page is yours on?" Cheryl asked as we headed out of customs.

"I think he put it on page three. It's my first one! I'm so excited!" Having the first "real" international stamps on our passports tickled us far more than it should. We must have looked like total goofs.

With customs cleared, our first challenge began. We couldn't figure out how to get out of the airport. Bleary-eyed and jet-lagged, we re-read the directions to the Dublin International Youth Hostel:

From Dublin Airport, get bus 16A/41/747 to Dublin, alight on the last stop on (just after the Temple Pub) Dorset Street. Turn right onto Blessington St, then left to Mountjoy St.

Sounded easy enough, right? Let's get to the bus. Ticket Advance Purchase Required, the sign said. We walked up and down past the bus ticket machines hoping to watch someone else use it first so we'd know if this was the right machine for the bus we needed. Signs were on each machine for transfers, all day tickets, and tickets for the busy time of the day, regular fares, and discounted times.

How were we to get tickets, the correct ticket, or even the required coins for exact change was a mystery still. American dollars and coins were out and euros were now our method of exchange. I didn't know yet that euros came in coin form. Our lack of traveling savvy was painfully obvious.

We just kept plodding along in front of the machines, hoping by osmosis the answers would come. Finally, Cheryl went off to ask for directions. I'm wandering around the airport with my hair sticking out at odd angles, eyes puffy from lack of sleep, a little drool stain on my shirt, and pushing a cart with about a hundred pounds of our luggage precariously perched on top of it. I'm sure quite the sight to anyone who slowed down enough to notice my zombie-like state. Thankfully, no one seemed to care.

4

"All journeys have secret destinations of which the traveler is unaware."

- Martin Buber

Dublin

We're in Dublin. The name rolls off the tongue. In my mind's eye, I'm seeing Irish fairies bringing rounds of steaming stew and pints of foamy Guinness in toasty warm spaces. We're toasting to other travelers and locals in pubs while making life-long friends in the process. What I didn't dream of was how cold and blustery it would be in the middle of summer. Forty-nine degrees – ouch! People walking by on the streets have umbrellas ripped out of their hands by the near hurricane-force winds. The rain is incessant, frosty, and bites deep into any exposed skin.

We stumble up the steps of the hostel with our backpacks weighing us nearly to the curb. Navigating the slippery steps with a soggy, rain-soaked pack wasn't an easy feat, but when we lurched through the door, I noticed two things immediately. It was gloriously warm inside. Ahh. Warm and dry. The second thing was the smell. An institutional, old orphanage, wet wool, World War hospital type of aroma – not entirely unpleasant, just quite different.

This being our first hostel experience – ever – we weren't exactly sure what the protocol would be. Young, lanky, bearded, and bespectacled hostel inhabitants were lounging on the sofas, reading in corners, and looking at magazines behind the desk. My immediate concern was that we would be turned away, back into the cold, lashing rain. It is called a *Youth* hostel, after all. Certainly, we were far too old to be staying here. The average age of anyone I saw was around twenty-one. With a good twenty years on the oldest, I was starting to be nervous. Looking at two bedraggled and decidedly older women, sagging under the weight of their belongings – would they send us somewhere else? An Irish Convalescent Home perhaps?

I needn't have worried. Sergio, a charming young Spanish man with a gorgeous smile we instantly fell in love with, jumped up from behind the desk and attended to getting us checked in. He didn't seem to notice our noses beet-red and eyes tearing from the cold or our misshapen, frozen fingers trying hard to hold on to our gear.

"Here are your linens," he smiled again and handed us a stack of white things. Sheets, pillowcase, and a towel – all starched stiff and blindingly white. For seventeen euros a night (about twenty-five dollars), we each have a bed in the women's dorm, fresh linens, and a continental breakfast to look forward to.

"Here is the key to Room 305. And here is a key to your lockers." The pile of things Sergio handed us grew higher. "You have bunks three and four. Your room is just up the stairs and down the hall." Up the stairs we went. Three flights. Bent over with the weight of our backpacks and a full set of bed linens, it wasn't a fast journey. We learned quickly that elevators were going to be a luxury of our past lives.

The Dublin International Youth Hostel was formerly a convent and school for girls. The old confessionals are now phone booths where I'm sure more than one teary-eyed traveler has owned up to past sins.

The stained-glass chapel area is now the dining hall and I admit to feeling a twinge of guilt when we shared late evening whiskey with some of the staff near the old pulpit. The dorm rooms bring to mind school days of long ago – high, echoing ceilings, creaky floors, cavernous spaces, and massive windows to entice young minds away from lessons being taught inside.

Lining both sides of our room were bare, blue, metal bunk beds. Bunk beds? This would be a first for me. Four sets of beds, so this room could hold eight people. "Any room with more than two beds in it isn't a hotel, it's a shelter," our friend Sandy had commented when we talked about staying in hostels and tried to convince ourselves how they weren't much different from hotels. Eight people in a room would take some getting used to.

I promptly called the top bunk. This upset Cheryl more than I'd expected.

"You can't sleep up there," she said.

"I didn't know you had a thing for top bunks."

"I don't. It's just that you…umm…you aren't the most coordinated person in the world. You might fall out during the night. And you're short. It's harder for you to get up there. It would be better if I took the top bunk."

"No way. I'll take it. I've always wanted to sleep on a top bunk." Shoving my pile of linens over my head, I clambered up the creaky metal bars serving as a ladder – needing only a small shove on my backside from Cheryl to push me over. Throwing myself on the bare mattress with a whump, it only then occurred to me I still had to make the bed.

Cheryl kept her head down, busily tightening up her own sheets with military precision. Only occasionally did she glance up at me with a grin as I rocked the bed frame and tousled sheets, trying my best to get tucked in while sitting on top of them. After a few miserable minutes, I gave up and took the help she offered.

Once the exhausting ordeal of making the beds was complete, we fell into our bunks and passed out. It didn't matter the mattress was only as thick as quarter or I had only one anorexic pillow or the bed squeaked and groaned with every movement – the sheets were fresh, clean, cool and lying flat was like sleeping on the finest fluffy duvet.

Sometime during our morning catch-up-on-jet-lag nap, we heard beds scraping and muffled voices whispering in the room. "They're still sleeping and it's almost noon. They must have been out drinking and partying very late last night."

Later we would meet our roommates from the Netherlands; Gesbertha and her daughter Nina, here to celebrate Nina's eighteenth birthday. At last, we meet someone our own age, even if it's another traveler's mother. Conversations were warm (especially after we explained the circumstances of our late morning lie-in) and we made our first friends at the hostel.

We learned of an odd Irish birthday tradition – to lift the birthday child upside down and give his or her head a few gentle bumps on the floor for good luck. The number of bumps should correspond to the child's age plus one. Deciding this tradition should probably stop when the child is no longer a toddler, the four of us choose to celebrate Nina's birthday with dinner and drinks at a local pub instead.

Dublin gets its name from Dubh Linn, which means Black Pool. The label refers to an ancient molasses-like lake in the city, which is now part of a penguin enclosure at the Dublin City Zoo. This we learned on our topless Hop-On, Hop-Off bus tour through the city. The bus was topless. We were wearing every piece of clothing we owned. While there were a few patches of blue sky shyly peaking out, it was still windy and bitter cold. Perfect weather for a visit to a pub.

The Irish have drinking down to an art form. The original Guinness Brewery in Dublin (and the number one tourist attraction in Ireland) carries a 9,000-year lease on its property, at a perpetual rate of forty-five Irish pounds a year. Only about eighty dollars US!

James Joyce once called Guinness stout the "wine of Ireland", and after a few thick, foamy, surprisingly warm pints – I was repeatedly toasting his immeasurable insight and trying not to fall off the barstool.

Even their famous Saint Patrick likes to get into the act. It's popular in Ireland to pin sprigs of shamrocks on your coat on Saint Patrick's Day in remembrance of shamrock leaves to illustrate the Holy Trinity. At the end of the day, one would "drown the shamrock" by putting a few into a glass and covering them with whiskey.

Those who drink to forget, please pay in advance!

I copied this bar sign on a coaster from a Public House on our last day in the city. It's smeared with mustard and has dribbles of beer smudging the words. It's still one of my favorite Dublin souvenirs.

Kilkenny

Our various duties and responsibilities on this trip were clear from the beginning. Cheryl is the planner. She's the one who books all our important details. This is for good reason. In the early stages of planning the trip, I found an on-line hostel site and booked a place for us in Ireland. This was exciting to me because it was haunted – a haunted hostel and an authentic 16th century Irish Castle to boot. Wow!

I'd tell anyone who would listen, "We're going to stay in a real castle in Ireland. And it's haunted, too."

Responses would range from, "Oh really, how nice," from the lady at the deli counter to "Why would you want to stay there? Can't you find a castle without ghosts?" from close friends. Their skepticism didn't matter to me a bit. This place was certified as haunted. A group from the BBC television show *Ghost Hunters* had stayed the night and their machines documented "the best ghostly sounds of any place they visited in Ireland". This was going to be awesome.

Mind you, I've never had much experience with ghosts, but this place sounded like a perfect place to stay in Ireland. A Norman castle from the 16th century, haunted by a young girl thought to have been banished for life to the high Tower room to prevent her from seeing the boy she loved – this was so Romeo and Juliet. And I'm a hopeless romantic.

Unfortunately, getting to the famous Foulksrath Castle wasn't as easy as we'd hoped. We'd had our fill of Dublin city life and were anxious to see a bit of the countryside we'd heard so much about. It should be simple. Foulksrath Castle was twelve kilometers from the town of Kilkenny and just a two hour bus ride from Dublin.

Off to find the bus. Again it was raining. Not just drizzling, but a full-force lashing rain met us as we tramped our monstrous backpacks down to the bus stop and unceremoniously tossed them under the bus in the already waterlogged luggage compartment.

When we arrived in Kilkenny, it was still pouring and the skies gave no sign this wasn't going to be an all-Sunday event. In seconds, we were soaked where we stood on the street. Sloshing around with a thirty pound backpack, a nineteen pound daypack with various computers and cameras, and yesterday's lunch leftovers wasn't much fun. It was a nightmare.

Our instructions provided by the hostel for getting to the castle seemed exceptionally clear: *Take the Orange Buggy. It runs all day.*

Jumping over streams of water running down the sidewalks, we headed for the taxi stand – only six blocks away. By the time we found the taxi, I was blind. My glasses were covered with water droplets and I wished for the invention of electric eyeglass-wipers.

"Aye, ye'll find the Orange Buggy over the other side of the road." The taxi driver pointed from inside his warm, dry car. We thanked him profusely, started to run to the other side, only to be called back. "Nay, today. The Buggy doesn't run on Sundays."

I know I was responsible for booking us at this place, but nowhere in the fine print did it mention the Orange Buggy didn't run on Sundays. Our helpful taxi driver said he'd take us to the castle for twenty Euros (about thirty-five dollars). Dripping wet and somewhere beyond rational thought, I agreed with Cheryl that it might be a good idea to stow our bags – now waterlogged and mushy – in the nearby tourism office, grab some lunch, and look around town a bit.

The tourism office was a bust. The rosy-cheeked receptionist couldn't have been nicer, but as she pointed out, "There is only a wee space in here for me self." She suggested we go to the train station "up the hill" as there is a left luggage area there. As we slipped and slid over cobbled streets, the train station seemed to grow farther away. After a half-hour's uphill soggy schlep, we arrived.

Putting down our packs on a dry spot inside the chilly train station was pure bliss. Finding out left luggage is closed on Sundays in Kilkenny was pure hell.

This time when I hoisted the backpack, I tossed yesterday's leftovers in the garbage. They were probably all squashed anyway. By this point, I'd lost all feeling in my fingers and toes. Life was looking pretty dismal right about then.

"Let's go find a pub. We'll bring our things with us and stow them inside. It'll be dry inside and we'll drink a pint or two to warm up."

She had me with the word "Let's". I was there. I was on my last frayed nerve and was getting more frustrated by the minute. The only thing keeping me from running screaming back down the street was the prospect of something good at the end of this soggy rainbow. I have to give Cheryl kudos for keeping the journey going past this miserable moment in Kilkenny.

We slogged back downtown and ducked into the first place we found. A glorious, balmy, stew-smelling bar with a lively wait staff that didn't blink twice when we bundled our mountain of stuff beside the table. It was heaven.

This was our first venture into the world of Irish sports, but by late afternoon we were cheering with the locals at Gaelic football on one screen and hurling on the other. When the rain finally eased and the afternoon shadows lengthened, we reluctantly asked our bartender if she knew the best place to get a reasonably-priced taxi to Foulksrath Castle.

She nodded, expertly pulled two pints of Guinness from the tap and motioned for us to follow her into a back room. She set the two pints in front of a gentleman, who judging by his empties on the table, had been there all afternoon. Putting herself between him and the hurling match he was watching, said "Seamus, look here. These girls need to get to Foulksrath. Take them there." He emptied his new pints with a speed that had me blinking in astonishment, nodded and said, "Aye, meet me in front in a minute. I'll bring the car right around."

Cheryl and I looked at each other and shrugged. We'd already downed enough pints so this suggestion didn't seem so farfetched. Our ride had been provided by Irish hospitality and who were we to question.

His alcohol tolerance was much higher than my own. By the time we arrived at the castle I was quite tipsy. Check-in time at the castle hostel was between five and seven PM – we were there just a little after six. The looming castle tower was imposing and the sense of foreboding as we walked through the afternoon gloom to the massive wooden doors kept growing larger. Low clouds were coming in from all directions to shroud the outbuildings from clear sight.

We knocked. And waited. The damp, cottony quiet was eerie. There wasn't another voice to be heard; except an enormous, raucous crow on a nearby electric line. We knocked again. And waited. I was seriously questioning my judgment in putting us in this remote, supposedly haunted place when the door opened and we were greeted by the shockingly white-haired, tousled caretaker – Jack.

"Welcome! Welcome!" Enthusiastically, he invited us inside. "Let's head up to the studio to get you checked in." Sharing a quick look of "what exactly have we gotten ourselves into" we hoisted our packs again. "My, you've got lots of baggage there. Just how long were you planning on staying?"

"Oh, just two nights," I added helpfully.

He looked over our bags with pity and said, "The dorm in the Tower is empty. You may have it all to yourselves – if you don't mind a little climb. Or you may have the dorm downstairs where there are already a few families staying."

The Tower sounded fine. The climb, wow, up a narrow, winding staircase that seemed to go on forever. As soon as we'd approach one landing there would be another farther on ahead. Candle-lit shadows followed us and the dampness from the castle walls made it feel as if we were camping in the clouds.

That night, lying on our bunks by light of kerosene lantern, we waited for it to happen – the first connection to a real ghost. The setting was perfect. Creaks and groans from the wind played a creepy prelude. The castle even smelled ghostly. Alas, we both fell fast asleep before noticing anything visiting from the spirit world. Or perhaps our psyches had already been so shaken up by our misadventures so far that the ghost took pity and let us sleep. Thank you ghost!

Killarney

As we walked the half mile from the bus stop, the sweeping front lawn of Killarney's International Hostel was filled with sun-seeking pale faces, happy dogs chasing Frisbees, and clusters of beer-drinking travelers settled on picnic tables. It would have been a delightful sight if we hadn't been suffering from gut-wrenching food poisoning and the bus we were walking from hadn't been our third of the day.

On waking up at Foulksrath Castle our last morning in Kilkenny, we both felt a little odd. Something was definitely haunting our insides. I was first to succumb to a full out run for the toilets when the smell of someone cooking breakfast hit my nose. This continued with rising frequency as we packed up our things and prepared to hike down to the bus stop in the drizzling rain – to the first of three buses we needed to get us to Killarney by afternoon.

I can't think of anything more miserable than trying to stifle the sounds of being sick in a plastic bag – on a bus – for six, long hours. Hoping not to gross out our fellow passengers too much, we found seats far away from everyone and tried to moan quietly. By the time we'd changed buses again, I'd estimated being sick at least six times. We were running out of plastic bags.

The bus passed through amazing countryside that if we'd been coherent would have taken our breath away. Rolling hills, craggy mountains, massive deer and sober, munching cows. Unfortunately, we had to ignore the sights and tried hard to close our eyes so the bus motion and swiftly flying-by scenery didn't add to our woes.

Our arrival in Killarney was met by a bright afternoon of sunshine – the first we'd seen in days. We didn't take too long to bask in it, however, as we were given our room key to the women's four bed dorm, sheets and pillowcase, and were pointed to a building outside. We promptly fell into our respective bunks, thankfully having the room to ourselves, and slept for the next twelve hours.

When I woke for the first time I wasn't sure where I was or even the time of day. Groggy and disoriented, I thought I'd been arrested. I was in a cell – in a bunk on a hard mattress. Sounds of other inmates were coming from the hallway. There was a single sink dripping in the corner and water-stained ceiling tiles above my head. What had I done? As my stomach started protesting against being woken from suspended animation, I realized what I had done. I was in a hostel.

Perhaps it was the ordeal of two days of food poisoning or maybe even the fact we'd stayed in three different hostels in the space of a week – but whatever the reason, I was quickly getting over sharing. In a hostel environment you share everything – the room to sleep in, the shower to bathe in, the kitchen to cook in, the laundry to wash clothes in, even the linens to make the bed. I grew up an only child and sharing has never been a big part of my life. Now I was being forced to share it all. Nothing here was mine, except a toothbrush and a few pairs of underwear. This concept – on top of being violently ill – was trying my traveling patience. And here we were, less than a week into our trip.

The first few days of hostelling, I had been in such giddy state. There was the excitement of being in a new place, seeing gorgeous vistas, and meeting stimulating people. The little things hadn't seemed like a problem. Now, lying on my back in the dark, listening to the incessant drip of the faucet, I felt miserable. I wanted to take a shower, but to do so meant lugging all my shower paraphernalia – soap, shampoo, shower shoes, and towel – into the shower with me. I imagine it would be strongly frowned upon for a forty-four year old woman to sprint naked down the hall to her room after taking a shower. This meant my clean clothes to change back into had to come with me, too.

All of this stuff – and me – had to fit in a space not much bigger than a phone booth. Knowing all the hostel inhabitants in this building shared these same two showers didn't do much for my worry of cleanliness. In the first few hostel showers, I'd be grossed out by dripping water I imagined someone else stepping in and a stray hair would put me over the edge. Though as time went on, I quit looking and just jumped in. It was the only way to adapt.

Cheryl was suffering too. The food poisoning had drained her energy and the sometimes non-existent schedules of public transportation were challenging her brilliant agenda planning skills. We knew what we wanted to see – the Ring of Kerry, Dingle Peninsula, Fungi the Dolphin, Irish castles and countryside, and of course, the quaint seaside pubs. Prices for motor coach tours were exorbitant – and even more importantly, we didn't want to be a part of the "tour bus" crowd. We were travelers for goodness sake. It was time to take action.

The young man behind the hostel desk gave us the chance we needed. We could have space, the freedom of not being on anyone's schedule but our own, and be able to see all the sights on our list. A rental car was the answer. They'd even deliver it to the hostel. The price was right (one day of car rental was the price of half of a single ticket by motor coach). It was a no-brainer.

The car was to be delivered the next morning. For the first time in several days, we were starting to feel normal again. We gleefully packed a picnic lunch (Irish soda bread, cheese, turkey, and jam) for the Ring of Kerry tour. We'd be setting out as soon as we were up and showered. Maps and guidebooks out on the table, we plotted each stop and charged all the camera batteries. Cheryl would drive and I would be the navigator. This was our first outing on our own in a foreign country. We were incredibly excited.

Pulling out of the driveway the next morning, I got a brief glimpse of perhaps why the convenience of a motor coach might be appealing. In Ireland, one drives on the left side of the road. All the tidbits related to driving – steering wheel, gear shift – are on the opposite side. In short, everything is exactly backwards from where you would expect it to be and all the motions of driving must be done in reverse. I climbed in the right side of the car, what I've always know to be the passenger side, only to be met with a steering wheel in my lap.

"I thought I'd be driving today. Did you want to drive?" Cheryl asked as she poked her head in.

"Oh no! I'm just in the wrong side of the car." How embarrassing.

Our first foray into town was a white-knuckled experience for me and one I'm sure when Cheryl wishes she'd brought along a blindfold and duct tape to muffle my screams. The tiny streets were not only occupied by whizzing cars, but also by any number of brightly-clad bicyclists and jaunting carriages (pony drawn traps with no fear of mechanized traffic).

On my side of the car – the side nearest the steep, drop-off cliffs – there were low, rock walls lining the roadway. Observant passenger that I am, I commented on these to Cheryl.

"I'm sure they were put there to keep us from falling off into the sea," she said.

I looked over in horror, but saw she was grinning, while trying to keep the car from a head-on encounter with another vehicle at 110 kilometers an hour. Looking back, I have no idea how we managed to avoid hitting either a speeding lorry, motor coach, or the beautifully constructed rock wall protecting us from a spectacular death.

The 180 kilometer (112 mile) journey called The Ring of Kerry is known for its magnificent and inspiring scenery. Craggy, sea-sprayed cliffs; boggy villages; and glorious meadows stretch out as far the eye can see – if the eye could actually see it. It was pouring rain. The slow, steady drizzle we'd woken up to had progressed into a full-blown sog-fest. Clouds hung so low it was impossible to see more than a few feet off the ground; but if we could see, I'm positive the views would be spectacular.

We had raincoats, wool socks, and a packed lunch looking for a picnic, so we did what most sodden travelers do – we got out and climbed mossy steps to the ruins of Ballycarbery Castle. Soon Cheryl was scrambling up ancient stairways, exploring every nook and cranny of the crumbling castle. While I tromped through the high grass; taking full advantage of the fact Ireland has no snakes – as I never allowed myself to tromp through high grass back home. I felt whisked back in time, imagining the legions of Braveheart crossing the sea in the foggy distance.

It was a day spent in historical exploration. Being from a country as young as the United States, sometimes it's hard to get the mind around a place like Staigue Fort. Mulling over a stone fort built over 2,500 years ago while trying not to fall off of the steep, stone-blocked sides would have been better suited for a less sloppy day.

At the Kerry Bog Village we were kissed by a Bog Pony – an adorable, blaze-faced creature whose hair was frizzing in the rain, just like ours. Studying the spaces inhabited by the blacksmith AND all the horses and cows in his tiny home gave living with a shedding dog a new perspective. The distinctive smell of peat fires in the hearth had us longing for the warmth of a roaring fire.

We drove back to Kilkenny for a few pints, a hot meal of lemon chicken pasta Cheryl prepared in the shared kitchen, and then a few games of cards in the common room. Here we shared tales of the day's adventures with other travelers at the hostel. My unpleasant woes of this journey eased with each passing hour.

Taking advantage of the freedom a rental car provided, our next day was to visit the Dingle Peninsula – a place I had such fun saying over and over.

"If you say Dingle one more time I'm going to strangle you," Cheryl said, never taking her eyes from the zooming cars on one side and the bicyclists on the other.

"Dingle. Dingle. Dingle. I love saying Dingle." I was trying to navigate us in the direction of one of the most spectacularly beautiful seaside villages in Ireland. Mother Nature was being kind – the clouds were rising and the extraordinary loveliness of the countryside was all around us. Rainbows were everywhere we looked. Mountains flowed into velvet green valleys so deep it was impossible to see the bottom.

This was a day of delightful wanderings. We found beehive huts incredibly entertaining – running from hut to hut, peeking out at the jaw-dropping panoramas and wondering what it would be like to live and work in such an inhospitable, but ruggedly gorgeous country. A last stop at another ring fort dating back to the Iron Age, over 5000 years ago! It was perched over crashing waves and vistas of blue and green so incredible a mere photograph wouldn't do it justice.

The Irish are known for their brilliant quotes and everyone has a favorite. While visiting this part of Ireland, I noticed many sayings seemed to have just enough truth to make one wonder.

An Irishman is never drunk as long as
He can hold onto one blade of grass and not
Fall off the face of the earth.

We had the pleasure of meeting the elderly gentleman for whom this particular quote was probably written. We were on the way back from our visit to Dingle in the early afternoon and stopped by a charming spot for lunch. Cheryl and I, with our new friend, were the only patrons at the pub. The proprietress pulled our beers and asked if we'd like some apple pie. I'd seen it on the counter as we came in – massive, flaky, warm and calling me.

"Aye, you should try her pie. It's the best around," Our bar mate agreed with the rumblings in my stomach. "You girls out mountain climbing today?"

It must have been our rappelling gear that gave it away. "No, we've just driven to Dingle. Enjoying the scenery," I answered.

"Ah, driving. Well, I'm a mountain climber myself. Like to get out most days. Especially one as nice as today."

One thing about Ireland, you'll never sit at a bar in silence as long as there is another body drinking beside you. Talking to people in pubs in a fun pastime and this fellow seemed interesting.

"So did you climb today?" Cheryl asked kindly. We were treated to an obvious rolling of the eyes from our bartender.

"Oh, aye. Aye," our friend said. "Nice climbing…." Then he wasn't there anymore. He'd disappeared in the middle of a sentence with a dreadful thump onto the wooden floor. I looked at the bartender in horror, expecting her to perhaps call an ambulance or at least look concerned, but she shrugged and said quietly, "He falls off all the time. He'll get up."

Sure enough, in a few seconds, the top of his head appeared over the bar. Shortly, the rest of him followed. He pulled himself up, took a sip of his pint, and continued the conversation as though he'd just come back from the WC. "Aye, a nice climb today. Got a leg cramp, though and had to call it a day." As he reached down to massage his calf, I held my breath he wouldn't pitch forward again.

Cheryl and I nodded with him. A few pints and a half hour later, he threw a few coins on the bar and stumbled out the door, leaving his sweater behind. Cheryl tried to get his attention, but the bartender waved her off, grabbing the sweater and running out the door.

"He won't hear you. He's on his way to another pub down the road. Watch the place for me for a minute while I go catch him. He'll be needin' this later on."

So here we sit, watching over the pub (and a fresh apple pie) in the magnificent County of Kerry. We had arrived!

5

"A good traveler has no fixed plan and is not intent on arriving."

- Lao Tzu

Brussels

Brussels became a seat-of-the-pants stop for us. We'd been scheduled for London, but a small bombing incident at Heathrow airport diverted us at the last minute.

"I'm not feeling comfortable about London right now. Where would you like to go instead?" Cheryl asked, sipping her coffee at the Danny Mann pub in Killarney. We were booked to fly out to London the next morning and the Wi-Fi connection we'd been so happy to find was spotty at best. My full Irish breakfast would have to wait while we rolled the dice.

"What about Amsterdam?" Although not on our original list, it did seem like an interesting place to put in for a few days.

"No, just looked there. The flights are outrageous. Where else?"

"Let me see a map." My black and white pudding and odd little egg were getting cold. "Here," I pointed, "let's go here."

"Belgium? Why Belgium?" she asked.

Shaking my head, and being considerate since Cheryl had only one cup of coffee so far; I didn't rub in the obvious. "Belgium? What's it known for?" I teased. "Chocolate! Waffles! And beer! Three of my most favorite things. Who wouldn't want to visit there?"

"I've never been to Belgium," Cheryl said. "But before this trip I'd never been to Ireland, either."

So it was decided. Brussels, Belgium would be our next stop.

And because I'd secretly ordered a round of Irish coffees to finish off our breakfast, Cheryl was most agreeable and suggested we stay in a hotel rather than a hostel this time. "You're going to love this," she said while typing, sipping, and eating her breakfast all at once. "The hotel Beau Site even advertises a mini-bar in the room."

I was thrilled. The flight time to Brussels was to be only an hour and a half. But, by the time we'd taken a bus from the hostel to the main station in Killarney, onward from Killarney to Cork, and finally another bus from Cork to the Shannon airport – we'd already had our fill of travel. And we hadn't even stepped on the plane yet.

We were also ready for the rain to stop. The backpacks were loaded underneath the bus with each change, so by the time we reached the airport, our packs were a muddy mess.

Once we arrived in Belgium, it was a forty-five minute bus ride from the airport to Gare du Midi, our main bus station. From Midi, we took the Metro to our stop for the street where the hotel was supposed to be – all while the rain was soaking us from head to toe.

Considering all of the connections we'd had to make during our day, travel had gone fairly well. But now, afternoon shadows were starting to crowd the sidewalks and the rain we'd so hoped to escape in Ireland had followed us with a vengeance.

"Listen," I said, stopping for a minute to look up at a grey, wet building. "Can you hear it?"

Cheryl slowly turned around, her enormous backpack sporting numerous waterfalls – all seeming to converge on the top of her head. "Hear what?" she sighed. "All I hear is water running into my ears."

"The funny squishing sound our shoes make on the sidewalk. Squish, squish, with every step. It's funny."

Evidently, Cheryl didn't share my humor. She turned back around in silence and onward we trudged up and down unfamiliar side streets. Squish, squish, squish…

We must have looked quite the sight – two dripping, exhausted, middle-aged backpackers carrying way too much gear, slogging down the street, gaping at the glorious storefronts on either side – Versace, Chanel, Cartier.

We passed sidewalk cafés, elegant boutiques, and warm restaurants with dry, happy people inside. We gazed upward and tried not to drown as elegant spires and graceful arches soared over us. Brussels is a gorgeous city, even in the rain. And we saw quite a bit of it from our lengthy ramble through the downpour, in circles, trying to find our elusive hotel.

The directions had seemed much easier when we took them from the internet. From the map, it looked as though we would get off the Metro right in front of our hotel. This was not the case.

One of the downsides to backpacking, we quickly learned, was the time it took us to get anywhere. Also, when you are carrying everything you own on your shoulders, you find pulling your back into permanent need for a chiropractor is a daily occurrence.

Finally, we found it! Only thirteen blocks from the Metro station. Ignoring the blatant look of disdain from the French-speaking receptionist, we dribbled rainwater on the guest register in our excitement. Then we tested the weight limit of the miniscule elevator by wedging our bedraggled selves and stuff in for the ride to our room.

"I can't move," I choked as a buckle of unknown origin poked me unmercifully in the kidney.

"Neither can I," Cheryl gasped for what little air was available. "Is it possible for this thing to go any slower?" After several agonizing minutes, the door finally opened and we tumbled out into the hallway.

It was a real hotel room – ah, the luxury. Diminutive by comparison to American hotel standards, but we didn't have to share it or the bathroom with anyone else. For that I was supremely thankful.

Wet, tired, and finally free of the ever-looming shadow of my albatross (backpack), I was eager to sample one of the pleasures Belgium is famous for – a strong Belgian beer. In this country there are 450 different varieties of beer, many with personalized beer glasses in which a particular beer, and only that beer, can be served. The shape of each glass is designed to enhance the flavor of its beer. Cheryl dug two cold Leffe's out of the mini-bar and with our hair still dripping, we had our first toast to Brussels – straight from the bottle.

While Ireland had wowed us with its pastoral beauty, Brussels was the first truly European city on our trip. We were captivated by the modes of transportation available: bicycles for rent you could simply pick up in one section of town and leave in another, motorcycles with a roof, and teeny Smart cars needing only a few inches to park. Nowhere to be seen were the massive SUVs and sedans driving everywhere in America. And the Brussels mass transit system was excellent for getting around the city.

Even with all the transportation options available, in three days we logged over ten miles on Cheryl's trusty walking pedometer. Exercise was an absolute necessity when breakfast every morning was a plate of warm croissants with chocolate hazelnut paste and apricot jam.

Chocolate fountains bubbling in the windows of sparkling stores weren't helping us reach our goal of losing weight on this trip – so we gave up and ordered a loaded Belgian waffle on the street. Almost a foot high, our work of art was a luscious layering of thick waffle, cinnamon, custard, strawberry, bananas, a small mountain of whipped cream, and chocolate drizzle. It was heavenly – sticky, sweet, and sinful.

Based on the astonished stares of several passer-bys, we might have enjoyed our feast just a little too much. Near the spot where we devoured the waffle, at the corner of the Rue de l'Etuve and the Rue du Chene, stands the fountain of Manneken Pis. That's Dutch for the "little pee man" in case you were interested.

This cherubic statue is adorable. Standing a lofty twenty-four inches from the top of his curly head to his chubby little toes, this naked fellow is one of Brussels' most famous landmarks. Bending his knees and smiling with glee, the Manneken Pis stands forever happily peeing into the fountain.

I expected him to be bigger and without thinking, muttered my disappointment within earshot of one of the shopkeepers lining the street. She tutted at me as though I had aimed an insult at an unattractive baby.

"Zee Manneken Pis is perfect," she said with dripping disdain. Leading me to row upon row of Manneken souvenirs ranging from playing cards to chocolate renditions of a peeing child, she pointed out a postcard of his costumes, which I felt obligated to buy to rescue my dignity for insulting the tyke.

He has over 760 different outfits to match special occasions in the city. Heads of state from visiting countries traditionally bring along a Manneken-sized version of their national costume. Some of his more popular attire includes Elvis, Mickey Mouse, Nelson Mandela and St. Nicholas.

The story of how Wee Manneken found a place to perpetually pee varies with who is telling it, but the story we liked spoke of a little boy saving the city from an enemy explosive attack by wetting the burning fuses. He managed this much in the same way he does it to this day.

The lucky little guy is often hooked up to a keg of beer and cups are given to people passing by during festivals. We were most disappointed to learn that during our visit there were no such festivals.

Eager to escape the hordes of tourists trading euros for junk, we scouted for a nice place to stop in for a drink. This was one pastime we seemed to have mastered. As we turned from a small side street – right in front of us – we'd stumbled upon the most singularly spectacular sight so far in our travels. The Grand Place to the French, or Grote Markt area to the Dutch.

It was a good two minutes before either of us spoke. Even then it was with such intelligent murmurings as "Wow!", or "Oh my God!", sprinkled with a few "Holy Cows!" for good measure. Our jaws simply refused to close. The place was stunning.

The Archduchess Isabella, daughter of Filip II of Spain, wrote about the square during her visit to Brussels on September 5th, 1599: "Never have I seen something so beautiful and exquisite as the town square of the city where the town hall rises up into the sky. The decoration of the houses is most remarkable." That's exactly what I would have said, too, if I could have formed a coherent sentence.

We were standing in an enormous square, dwarfed by Baroque Guild houses and government buildings covered with magnificent sculptures – stern knights, soldiers, priests, saints, and heroes – not one of whom we could identify on sight, but all must have been remarkably famous in their time.

We did recognize the statue of the Archangel Michel, the patron saint of Brussels, on top of the magnificent Hotel de Ville de Bruxelles. On the Maison du Roi, so many eyes, frozen in time, were watching our every move. Then there were the gargoyles – my personal favorite – sharing space with ivy-crusted gilded pediments decorated with baskets flowing with petunias.

It was almost more than the senses could absorb. After an hour or so of gawking, we finally managed to pull away. Not far, mind you. We ducked into a small café for a beer and to people-watch in the square.

My stomach rumbling from taking in this majesty, not to mention two strong beers on an empty stomach, it was time to find dinner. Off we went in search of the Sacred Isle. Romantic, cobbled, winding streets lined with every type of restaurant imaginable – so inviting. If the waiters weren't pushing so hard to get patrons to choose "their" spot, it would be much more fun to browse.

Gigantic, iced displays of shrimp, lobster, clams, and delicious moule (mussels) were vying for street space with the placards advertising the specials of the night. It wasn't a tough choice for me. I'd been searching for moule frites (mussels and French fries) since we'd arrived. Cheryl's not a seafood eater, but ordered an amazing steak au poivre she was kind enough to share a bite of. Waddling back to our hotel, we were forced into just one more stop at the Manneken Pis Truffle House. The lightly dusted gingerbread truffle I popped into my mouth almost had me in tears.

The next morning, we were up and out to take in as much as we could while the sun was shining. It was a day for the Hop-On, Hop-Off Tour Bus. We visited many sights of the city, sitting high atop the double-decker, covered in rain gear for the occasional downpours.

Something bothered me deeply about Mini-Europe Park. The Atomium – a 335 foot high representation of a molecule's nine atoms, magnified 165 billion times – was spectacular. Built for the World Fair in 1958, the enormous, shiny spheres connected by escalators provide some of the best views of Brussels. Being dwarfed by the Atomium wasn't what felt weird. It was the miniature versions of everything else – three hundred of Europe's most recognized and famous monuments, including the Eiffel Tower and the Acropolis. I felt as though I was visiting the island of Lilliput.

Touted as the place to go "if you can't see all of Europe in one trip", I imagined people going back home with their vacation pictures and telling friends, "I wasn't able to see the actual Coliseum in Rome, but I saw the miniature in Brussels. I'm sure it's the same. Now I can cross a place off my bucket list." This takes all the fun out of traveling, not to mention drawing a foul for trying to avoid the heat, admission fees, and crowds at the real sights.

The last night in Belgium, I spent enjoying the luxury of a hotel bed and trying not to get too upset at the sight of our drying socks and underwear stretched over laundry lines. With our undies blanketing the shower and bathroom doorway, I was coming to terms with what this trip really meant. Moving out of my normal comfort zone was such an understatement. It was also an act I had vastly underestimated.

"Only three sets of underwear – surely no one needs more than that, right?" I remember thinking just a few weeks before. Now it made me sad. Except for what I was wearing right then, my entire wardrobe could fit in a small pile at the end of the bed. I was already bored by my bland choice of colors: khaki, brown, beige, taupe, and a catalog-color called rust, simply another shade of brown. There was no extravagance of deciding which pair of shoes to wear with an outfit – I only had two.

Material possessions meant so much to me, I hate to admit. I am a collector of things – books, especially. Now all I carried was a ragged paperback I'd picked up at the hostel in Ireland. Brochures became my reading fix and I devoured them with the same speed and enthusiasm I'd gone through moule frites every night since we'd arrived in Belgium.

"I'm not sure how much longer I can do this," I confided to Cheryl as we were starting to pack up our things and head to yet another country.

"Do what? Traveling? Aren't you enjoying yourself?" Cheryl was embracing this whole trip with an eagerness I hadn't expected, but should have known given her typical good-nature.

The problem wasn't one of my not having a great time. Every single day was spectacular, amazing, something new and exciting, totally remarkable. What I hadn't expected was for it to be quite this hard. It had rained so much the past three weeks I felt as though a light coating of mold must be growing over my skin. A lingering chill had invaded my thin Florida blood. The idea of hoisting the heavy backpack on my shoulders one more time and lugging it around for weeks filled me with a deep dread. Damp clothes, strange beds, food I wasn't familiar with…whine, whine, whine. I was such a baby.

"I think I know how you feel," Cheryl said sympathetically. I looked over quickly – was this a trap? Cheryl didn't ever linger on the dreadful details. She was always on the positive side. Could she possibly be feeling as miserable as I was?

Her solution was better than my idea of catching the next flight back home. "Why don't we rent a car while we're in France? We can stow our packs in the trunk, go at our own pace, and take some time to see more of the countryside than if we're always at the mercy of train and bus schedules."

She's so smart! I'm so glad she's on this trip. Newly energized by the "car rental" idea, I couldn't wait to get going. This would solve all of our problems. We'd be driving a car! A car to protect us from the rain and to keep us warm – a car to carry my bloated backpack for me – a car to get us exactly where we wanted to go. If I'd had any idea at the time just how wrong the last statement would prove to be, I'm not sure I'd have been so ecstatic. But, you know what they say about hindsight.

6

"Twenty years from now you will be more disappointed by the things you didn't do than by the ones you did do. So throw off the bowlines, sail away from the safe harbor. Catch the trade winds in your sails. Explore. Dream. Discover."

- Mark Twain

PARIS

It was only an hour and a half train ride from Brussels to Paris, but that small distance was enough to tear us forcibly from the imagined safety and naivety of travel we'd been experiencing so far. Ireland and Belgium had spoiled us. The people were friendly and we trusted they meant us no harm. It was the all-important traveler's mistake of letting our guard down, even for a second.

As we exited the train at the Paris Gard du Nord, the skies were a brilliant blue. It seemed we'd finally escaped the rain rusting our hinges since Ireland. We would be staying at a Marriott hotel, using the last vestiges of Cheryl's old life as a Corporate Director to secure a free room for three nights on the Rive Gauche. The magic of Paris awaited and the possibilities seemed endless.

As we exited the RER B at the Denfert-Rochereau station, I struggled through the head-high, tight turnstile, backpack on shoulders and daypack in tow. I was barely through, when I heard Cheryl shout, "Hey, stop it. Hey!" and then a second later she appeared through the turnstile beside me.

"He took my wallet!" She yelled and tried without success to get back through. In mere seconds, this man had come up behind her and shoved her tight against the gate. Her first thought was he was trying to crowd in behind her to avoid paying, but she felt him reach into the Velcro pocket of her pants leg and pull out her wallet, then shove her forward. She was shouldering her own backpack, so the momentum carried her through the gates and when she turned around, he was running back and disappearing through the crowds coming down the stairs from the arriving trains.

Shouting after him in English did no good and neither did trying to call Metro security on the phones provided by the tracks. Our French wasn't good enough to communicate the urgency and the deafening sound of rushing trains drowned out what little could be understood from the conversation. Our biggest worry about Paris had been that we might encounter a bit of a language barrier – we simply didn't count on it coming into play so quickly. Or having to find the words in French to yell a pickpocket's description over the phone.

In a quick, shaky assessment, we determined Cheryl's wallet contained two credit cards, twenty-five dollars in US bills, forty euros, her US drivers license, a phone card, and some e-mail addresses from folks we'd met in Ireland. Her passport was safe in another spot and I had other cash and credit cards we could use.

"It could have been worse," we kept repeating. It was as much to convince ourselves it was true, as it was to help ease the feeling of violation we'd just encountered.

Cheryl blamed herself for letting her guard down. For putting the train ticket back into her wallet in plain view. For letting someone crowd her into the turnstile. All normal things anyone would do. Only this time, someone was waiting to take advantage of her vulnerability and pounce on it. I could tell she was visibly upset by this and there were no words I could find to help her.

"I just want to go home," she said quietly as her tears of frustration refused to slow down. "And right now I don't have a home to go to."

By the time we reached the hotel, we were both pretty shaken up. The blue skies didn't seem so appealing now and every stranger who bumped by was a potential thief. At the hotel, in the process of cancelling the credit cards, another shock was waiting.

"No, the last charges I made on the card were in Brussels, not in Paris. I've only just arrived in Paris," Cheryl explained on the phone at a long distance rate of two euros per minute. It seems our sticky-fingered friend was quite a pro. In the time it had taken us to get to our hotel (about thirty minutes), he had racked up over $3000 dollars worth of purchases. I had to laugh as I heard

Cheryl say, "Clothes? He bought $3000 in clothes? I don't spend that much on my wardrobe in a year!"

While the experience gave us an initial chill on Paris, those we dealt with in the aftermath were most gracious. The hotel concierge suggested we file a police report and guided us to the station. American Express responded with another card at their local office within two hours, and the police were sympathetic and patient, though they explained this was a frequently occurring scenario.

"What about the security cameras?" Cheryl asked. She'd noticed them all over the station, one in particular near the spot where her wallet was lifted. The police captain just shrugged. "It happens all the time. We are not able to keep up with the thieves. We can only warn tourists to be careful." We had our warning and vowed to be more watchful in the future.

Cheryl found small luggage locks and soon our daypacks were as tight as Wells Fargo – or so we believed. Bastille Day crowds were enormous in the city with thousands of people jostling about to celebrate and enjoy the beautiful weather. Still trusting public transportation to be the best mode of travel – we had locks on our bags after all – it was time to explore.

Denfert-Rochereau was the closest Metro station to our hotel (and the station where we'd been robbed the day before), so warily we descended the steps to our train. Oops, wrong side of the tracks. I was navigating again, after all. We would need to get to the other side of the tracks to get to downtown Paris.

Up the stairs we went, our backtrack coinciding with a massive rush of bodies from the train just arriving. Cheryl had me go ahead of her on the stairs because I typically don't pay too much attention to what was going on around me and this time carried our only credit cards in my wallet. Not to mention her rapidly growing distrust of all humanity.

This time I heard her voice loud and clear. "Stop it! What do you think you're doing?"

I whirled around and a hooded teenager was standing over a small bag on the steps just below Cheryl.

He'd come up behind her and unzipped the only pocket on her daypack not locked down tight. Only this time the joke was on him. The baggie he'd pulled out of her pack only contained a few feminine hygiene products. He'd dropped it like a hot potato. From the look of surprise on his face, this was the closest he'd come to these before.

"Do you need those, little girl?" Cheryl jeered back at him. He and his two young cohorts just laughed and ran back down the stairs against the flow of bodies. Warning from the police or not, it had happened twice in two days. In Paris, at the same station. All we wanted was to get even. Well, Cheryl was ready to leave Paris right then and there, but…

While sharing a carafe of wine in the afternoon, we came upon the perfect plan. A giant old-fashioned mousetrap (the kind capable of breaking the neck of a good-sized woodchuck), set in the same pocket of Cheryl's pack, half-zip it up, and wander through the station absentmindedly reading a map. It took a bit of the edge off imagining a loud "SNAP" followed by an even louder yelp. While we never got the chance to put our plan into play, it made us feel better thinking up ways to get back at the people who made us feel so violated.

"You know, I think I'm over public transportation for a while," Cheryl said at dinner, "it's time we rented a car." In Belgium, while I'd been busy complaining about how miserable I was lugging around a backpack, Cheryl had been doing what she does best – research. While she might not be saying it out loud, she was just as frustrated as I was with the backpack situation and being totally dependent on mass transit schedules. She'd been looking at the costs of renting a car for the remainder of our trip.

While renting a car for a few months to drive around Europe would be way beyond our allotted travel budget, there was another possibility. Both Peugeot and Renault had buy back" programs in which you purchased the car from them and sold it back once you were finished. Purchasing a car while traveling sounded like an impossible thing to me, but Cheryl was determined to figure out a way.

The Peugeot Open Europe Plan was what she found. Essentially you agree to "buy" the car for only the time you will use it. For us it would be sixty-seven days with a brand new Peugeot 207 Executive Diesel car, costing us a total of $1950. Not being one to throw away money at frivolous expenses, Cheryl did thorough research to compare the cost of getting this car versus our original plan of using public transport.

"Having the car will be less expensive than getting train or bus tickets everywhere and will let us get to places we might not be able to if we depend completely on the transportation available."

I was sold! This meant no more dragging around a huge backpack in the rain anymore. Life was looking great.

"We'll pick up a rental car while we're in Paris and keep it for nine days while we do the paperwork to get a car of our own. We'll pick up the new car in Nice and return to Paris when we fly back to the states."

What an awesome concept! The cost of $1950 included all required insurance and dropping off the car in a different location than we picked it up. It was as simple as applying on the Internet, signing papers in Nice, and driving away in a brand new vehicle. Getting this car changed the entire European experience for us.

With that settled, now it was time to enjoy Paris. This was the city I'd been dreaming about. To much rolling-of-the-eyes by Cheryl, I planned my own personal Hemingway Paris Pilgrimage. I have to admit my alter ego is a certifiable Ernest Hemingway stalker. I've visited his home in Key West, his grave in Ketchum, sat at the bar he frequented on Duval Street, studied his works, petted his six-toed cats, and mostly admired the larger-than-life character epitomized in American literature.

The idea of spending time in the very city where he wrote and drank gave me pleasure chills. I'd memorized the "Hemingway Tours" on-line and had copious notes of the places I wanted to visit. Sites immortalized by Papa: Shakespeare and Company, Marche Rue Mouffetard, Les Deux Magots, and Café Pre aux Clercs.

Paris possesses a current of creative energy running though it as deep as the River Seine. Artists, writers, musicians, and sculptors have lovingly called this city home and it's easy for me to see why. The monuments, cathedrals, pace of life, and people on the streets call to the artistic spirit. I was ready to sit down in a café, write for hours, and feel the power flow around me.

It was in Paris where I came close to finding what it was driving me to take this trip in the first place. Somehow pondering one's existence while sitting at a sidewalk café sipping a carafe of wine, nibbling mouth-watering French cheeses seemed to make perfect sense here. What drove us to leave the comfort of everything we knew and travel? There seemed as many reasons as pigeons begging in front of Notre Dame.

I was searching inside for what prompted me on this journey in the first place – looking for excitement or adventure, or to escape boredom? Maybe a little of each? I felt a connection to Paris deeper than any destination so far. It's in the air here. The ghosts are here. I can especially sense them as the bottle of Vin Rouge slowly empties and the streets crowd with silhouettes. Breezes blow over the Seine and coffee cups clink in the bistros of times gone by. Close your eyes and experience the exuberance of students as they argued over politics and danced to the beat of a revolution brewing in their hearts. Art blossoms in every corner. Today the moped replaces the carriage, but the impression is still the same – energy just under the surface, waiting to be tapped.

Cheryl wasn't so sure. She still stung from the pickpocket episode and every place we visited was tainted with worry it could happen again. On edge because of the robbery, always looking behind her, and ultra-sensitive to her surroundings – she was spooked by much different ghosts than those I sought.

"Let's take a day and be total tourists," I offered, reading from a brochure I'd picked up at the hotel. "The Hop-On, Hop-Off Bus is great here. Four routes through the city for one ticket. How about the Paris Grand Tour? Or Montparnasse-Saint Germain? We can see the Bastille from the top of a bus and not worry about pickpockets today. What do you think?"

I wanted her to enjoy Paris as much as I was and as a bonus, we could use the bus tour to mark a place on the map and come back there later. By the second day, we were getting to be quite the experts – like, which seats had the tightest holes to poke in the earphones so it wasn't hour upon hour of jiggling to hear the voices.

"Can you hear anything? Mine's not working. Change seats with me," I pleaded.

"What? I can't hear you."

"Is the man speaking in your ears?"

"I can't hear you. I'm listening to the man talking about Paris. Shhh." And so it went.

Giving our sore ears a break from the Open Tour Bus, we decided to take a break for lunch. We'd been very good so far, avoiding all the clichéd American food establishments, instead opting for local restaurants and markets. But an advertisement on the bus map caught my eye. And it was the coupon that sealed it.

"Cheryl, look! We can get a Free Hot Fudge Sundae with any purchase. We *need* this!" I cried as we neared Boulevard Montmartre. The Hard Rock Café beckoned us like a blue spring in the dessert. Yes, the beers were seven euros and the cheeseburger was thirteen ninety-five. Way over our budget, but today it didn't matter. We could read every word on the menu. The wait staff understood every word we said. And without butchering the language, we could order comfort food in the presence of other tackily dressed tourists and not feel a bit out of place. Here Cheryl seemed to relax for the first time since we'd arrived in the city. It felt familiar here. Comfortable. Well worth the price of a seven euros beer.

Now stuffed with gobs of chocolate sundae, we needed to get off the bus and get some real exercise. The Basilique du Sacre-Coeur provided just the incentive. Climbing the 402 very steep steps to the top of the dome provided an incredible view of Paris – the 402 steps back down provided incredibly sore calf muscles the next day. I could imagine the monks silently making the trip up and down several times a day to ring the bells, wearing the steps glassy from thousands of feet slipping over them.

Basilique du Sacre-Coeur translates to the Basilica of the Sacred Heart. Found on the highest point in the city on the hill of Montmartre (Mount of Martyrs), legend suggests the location of the church is where Saint Denis, the first bishop of Paris, was beheaded in the third century. After the beheading, Saint Denis proceeded to bend down, pick up his severed head, and walk with it in hand many miles to the North. Finally, he rested at the place where the city of Saint Denis is found today. I'm already impressed by the pluck of these Parisians.

We learned many saints have come in pilgrimage to this holy site over the centuries: Saint Germaine, Saint Clotilde, Saint Bernard, Saint Joan of Arc, Saint Vincent de Paul, Saint Ignatius of Loyola, and Saint François-Xavier. As with many sites we visited in Paris, I was moved to a state of goose-bumps for most of the day.

Since we already held a prime viewing spot on the hill of Sacre-Coeur, it was there we decided to watch the City of Lights really show off. As twilight started to swathe the panorama at ten o'clock, the twinkling began. The spectacle of an immense Paris skyline spread out as far as the eye could see.

We believed we'd seen so much from the bus – little did we know. The Eiffel Tower shimmered as though covered by moving diamonds – so fast it was difficult for the eyes to take it all in. The view was spectacular and the bottle of Grand Sud we'd bought for two euros capped a perfect day in Paris. My biggest lesson for the day? It's possible to buy a good bottle of French wine cheaper than buying a Diet Coke. I do love Paris!

It was time to leave the comfort of our Marriott Rive Gauche and move on to a more humble (and affordable) place to stay in Montmartre. Though staying in the shadow of the glorious Sacre-Coeur can hardly be considered a hardship. I did get a chuckle imagining the look on the faces of the cleaning staff in our 370 euros a night room when they opened the bathroom door to find a makeshift clothes line covered with our freshly washed, meager collection of clothes. It wasn't that we preferred hand-washing clothes. We simply couldn't fathom paying four euros to have one piece of underwear done at the hotel when we had washing supplies in our backpacks. The money would be much better spent on two bottles of wine!

The Hotel Utrillo proved to be a perfect base camp for wandering through the winding, bohemian artist community of Montmartre. The morning we spent in a pastime I'm a bit embarrassed to admit I enjoy – exploring old cemeteries. This one, the Cimetiere Montmartre, is a jewel. Here is the final resting place for Hector Berloiz, Dalida, Edgar Degas, and so many more whose names I write down to look up later. I know it sounds creepy to take pleasure in the streets and sepultures of a place where others are buried; but seeing the artistic sculptures, famous names, ironwork, the dedications, tributes, and expressions of devotion gives me faith in the future.

While wandering through the leaf-strewn pathways, I heard a kitten crying as though it was being tortured. Tiny, with eyes not quite open yet, this little one had somehow gotten far from its frantic mother. We found her peeking out the door of a weathered crypt. Picking it up and putting it closer to the tomb, we waited. In just a few minutes the momma swooped in, nabbed the mewling bundle, and with a one leap disappeared through the wrought iron tomb window. With our charge safely tucked inside, we headed back with a smile to rejoin the world of the living.

Our last night in Paris we keep the window open to listen to sounds from the street below. The breeze is cool. Traffic hums, airplanes drone, and French expletives from a passerby simply add a more human touch. Coughs from faceless shadows. A television in the distance broadcasting words neither of us understands. A lyrical flute plays from the garage across the street, the music sweet through the window. Someone puts out their garbage. A child being told to go to bed. A tiny corner of Paris sleeps and finally, so do we.

7

"The real voyage of discovery consists not in seeing new landscapes, but in having new eyes."

- Marcel Proust

Mont St. Michel

You can't imagine the sense of freedom we felt driving out of Paris in our own vehicle. No longer were we at the mercy of train or bus schedules. We could go where we wanted, when we wanted. The open road waited with nothing but an endless horizon to discover. It was pure bliss for about twenty minutes. That's how long it took for Cheryl to realize there was no radio in the car. It hadn't been removed. It wasn't there at all.

"No radio?" she sputtered. "How can a car not have a radio?"

"S'okay. We'll just have to talk to each other."

The look of horror on her face should have clued me in. I guess you think you know someone pretty well when you've been friends for over ten years, but I had forgotten how bad Cheryl's music addiction had become. Snippets of driving with her back in the States flashed through my mind. Constantly changing stations to find the perfect song, talking back to the little people inside the radio, and my favorite – she taunts it; "You're talking too much. I want music!" then smugly changes the channel.

Only slightly appeased we'd have this radio-less car for two weeks until we picked up our Open Road Peugeot in Nice; Cheryl tried hard to endure the void of music. And to be truthful, silence wasn't such bad thing. As miles piled behind us, we talked about where we'd been and now where we were going. The road ahead was full of unseen possibilities.

Our next destination, the Abbey of Mont St. Michel, was a few hours from Paris. The picturesque villages we passed through along the way were nothing short of a suspension in time. Stone cottages frozen forever, dripping with colorful petunias, sharing narrow roadways with pony carts, tiny inns, and café's. Soaking it all in took away most of ours words, except an occasional "gorgeous", "amazing", or "wow!" exclamation.

We arrived in the early afternoon at our first Bread & Breakfast on the journey. Named Au Bon Accuel, the 200 year old stone cottage near the Brittany/Normandy border exuded country charm. It didn't seem as though a car should be in the picture here, the entire place taking us a giant step backward to another era. Rock walls, well-worn farming tools, flower gardens, and vegetables growing fresh on the vines were situated just outside the kitchen window.

One of the perks of travelling in the manner we were is having interesting conversations with people along the way (unless they're trying to talk to me on an airplane!). Steve and Liz, the owners of this B&B, were no exception. Explaining their need to finally escape the working life in England and make a new start in this tiny village, Steve said, "It was difficult at first, but once we started advertising as a hostel and accepting "travelers" instead of "vacationers", we noticed such a difference. The travelers were so much happier and more accommodating, while some families here on holiday couldn't seem to leave the stress of their lives behind. They were trying too hard to push a year of vacation into a one week holiday. And weren't having any fun."

A happy escape from a life of stress was a topic Cheryl enjoyed talking to him about. Then Liz suggested if we wanted to avoid stress of our own, we might want to visit the Abbey now in the late afternoon, as most of the tour buses would be leaving for the day.

It was a great suggestion. Over four million visitors come to Mont St. Michel each year and the vast majority gets off a bus. As we drove down the quiet farm roads of St. Marcan toward the bay, we experienced a whisper of the history preceding us. Then in the distance, there it was – The Rock! I'd seen pictures in books and on a National Geographic special once, but nothing compared to seeing in person The Abbey of Mont St. Michel rise up from the water. You could truly see it from ten miles away!

Cheryl whispered reverently, "It doesn't look real. Like a city in space or something from Star Wars." And it did. Sitting out in the bay of the English Channel, rising up so high it seemed to touch the clouds. As we drove closer, the tidal flats surrounding the Abbey brought to mind a vast desert, extending in all directions as far as we could see. The tide was out and the musky, pluff mud smell smacked us as we rolled down the windows.

"Ahhh," I sighed. Growing up in Charleston, South Carolina, my nose was predisposed to savor and enjoy the stinky aroma of the ebbing tide.

"Pe-ew!" Cheryl chimed. Being born in Massachusetts, her nose wasn't as seasoned to the bouquet of salty brine and rotten eggs.

The smell wasn't the only thing assaulting us. Giant mosquitoes swarmed our little car, practically carrying it away. I've never seen mosquitoes so big before in my life. Batting them around inside the car hardly fazed the suckers and I worried one of the windows would break from the struggle.

We were now trapped in the car with windows rolled up tight. I wanted to take pictures of the vista stretching out before us – the medieval Benedictine Abbey of St Michel. The sun was setting and the colors seeping from the sky were breathtaking.

"Other people are outside and the mosquitoes don't seem to be bothering them." I said more to convince myself than Cheryl.

"Go for it then. I'll wait for you here in the car," was what I think she said. It was hard to recognize exact words over the plunking sound the enormous bugs made as they committed insect suicide against the windshield.

I made a mad dash into the marsh with my camera, catching the last golden glow of light on the water as the moon rose and pinpricks of candlelight in the Abbey started to appear. The huge, itching welts on my legs were worth the trouble and as the sun sank into the tidal flats, so did the horde of bloodsuckers.

Around the Abbey, there is a fifty meter difference in spring tide levels. This presents a difficult and dangerous trek for pilgrims to get to and from the mainland. It's much easier today because of the road, but in the past the pilgrims faced many perils. Whether because of the tides, quicksand, or thick mist (capable of enveloping the Abbey in minutes); the pilgrim's march is indeed a test of faith. But many try – as this is the fourth largest pilgrimage site in the world, after Jerusalem, Rome, and Santiago de Compostela.

I was careful to avoid the quicksand and the rising tides. Thankfully, the impenetrable fog was absent while we visited. Our guide explained in the event it appears, the Abbey rings bells to help lost souls find their way to the church. The next day, we found lost souls aren't the only ones who find their way to Mont St. Michel. Tourists by the thousands unloaded from the snaking line of tour buses coming in from the causeway. Within a few hours, it was wall-to-wall people.

Our only escape was to go up. We climbed to the Abbey Church, on top of the rock, two hundred forty feet above sea level. It seemed a lot higher after all those steps! The views across the bay? Absolutely magnificent! Gazing up at the gilded statue of Saint Michael on the Abbey steeple, we felt like pilgrims in our own right. Searchers for a deeper meaning in the lives we once knew.

Blois

The narrow, sun-flower ringed roads through the Valley of the Kings were scattered with glorious royal chalets perched along the Loire River. Names like Chambord and Cherverny rolled off the tongue as we passed castle after massive castle, their reflections glittering on the water.

"I think we've been by this one before," I said helpfully.

"Not possible. According to the directions, we're southeast heading toward Blois."

"Maybe you're right. All these castles do look alike. What time is it getting to be anyway?" I was now studying the map with more interest because I had to go to the bathroom and soon. We'd left Mont St. Michel around two PM and according to the directions, it should be about a three hour drive.

"Almost eight-thirty, but we should be close. Check the address again."

"Should be just up this street. But this looks like a residential area. Are you sure the hostel's here?"

"All I know is what Hostel World gave me," Cheryl barked. She was getting tired and cranky from being in the car, too. "It sounded nice on the Internet.

They advertised a shared kitchen, laundry facilities, even a restaurant. I'll be a good home base for a few days while we explore Blois."

"Okay, just up ahead. This should be the place…" Both of us stared in silence as it came into view. A high, chain-linked fence, topped by rows of barbed wire, surrounded the flat, graffiti-decorated buildings. Darkness enclosed the complex and there was no sign of movement anywhere. I whispered, "I think it's a prison."

"Uh-huh," she whispered back. It was all she could muster after driving in circles all day. I, on the other hand, picked this time to throw a fit.

"We can't stay here," I whined.

"Where else are we going to stay? It's almost nine. We're tired, hungry, and you have to go to the bathroom. And we're running out of clean clothes. We have to stay here. Let's just try to find a place to park and bring our stuff in. We'll make the best of it for one night." Always the voice of reason. But I wasn't ready to be agreeable just yet.

"There is no place to park. We've got to walk a mile." So maybe not a mile, but with my lumpy backpack filled with dirty clothes and the assorted other things I'd collected the past few days (like andouille sausage and shrimp for the wonderful pasta I'd planned to cook tonight in the shared kitchen); I was stumbling through the parking lot at a pretty slow pace.

By the time I got to the reception, Cheryl was trying unsuccessfully to communicate with the student behind the desk. Terms like "reservation" and "room" weren't being understood, even with the help of the English-to-French phrasebook and many flamboyant hand gestures.

He was patient and smiling, which in the state we were in, accounted for quite a lot. Despite the language difficulties, we secured a room and asked where we might find the shared kitchen, as my cooler bag with the shrimp and sausage was starting to emit a slightly odd odor.

A blank, but smiling, stare met us.

"The kitchen? La cuisine?" We spoke slowly in case speed was the issue.

He shook his head, pointed to the sign on the wall, and then went back to the book he was studying. The sign read in three languages: *Restaurant. Hours 8am – 8pm.*

"Non," we tried again, "la cuisine? The kitchen?"

Again, he pointed to the sign. "La cuisine est fermée." The kitchen is closed. We sighed (because by then it would be far too easy to cry), hoisted our backpacks, and tried not to notice the puddle of shrimp and sausage juice dribbling from my cooler bag.

Once you got over the bars on the windows and the view of the concrete basketball court where I imagined the inmates were allowed for their hour of daily recreation, the room wasn't too bad.

It reminded me of a college dorm. It even came with the requisite desk by the window. We piled our stuff on the desk and noting the smell radiating from the cooler bag, decided our first task was to find ice to keep the shrimp happy. I'm not sure what we were thinking. In the States, ice is available everywhere. I never realized just how common ice was in my life until I came to Europe.

Europeans recoil when asked for ice. It's not as though I'm asking to put catsup on the bouef bourguignon – I'd just like a bit of frozen water to chill my drink or my once-frozen, rapidly thawing shrimp. A quick look around the Institution led us to the "shared kitchen" as advertised on-line. Now we understood why the reception hadn't been eager to point us in this direction. It was a small room with a one burner hotplate sporting a frayed electrical cord. No refrigerator. No oven. No pots, pans, or utensils.

I almost cried as the realization started to set in. It wasn't happening. The shrimp and the sausage would have to go in the rubbish bin. Preferably far away from where we were sleeping. Cheryl volunteered to find a far-away trash receptacle and I took the task of cleaning out the now-reeking-of-shrimp-juice cooler bag. Cheryl's not fond of seafood smells on her best days, so her expression when coming back into the room pretty much summed up our experience so far that day.

"Sorry," I said, wrinkling my nose in sympathy. "I've opened the windows. The smell should be gone soon."

She sat on the bed as tired and dejected as I'd seen her so far this trip. There was only one thing to do. Pull out all the stops. We were in France after all.

I'd kept a bottle of good Burgundy in my bag from Paris for a special occasion. We had small plastic cups and even found two canned tuna salads and crackers with little spoons inside. We set up our little feast on the desk and watched the swallows swooping over concrete with a heat lightning fireworks display in the background. The room was sparkling clean and the sheets crisp and cool. We were both asleep before the bottle of wine was half empty.

When I woke up, the sun was shining and the familiar sound of Kenny Chesney singing "French-kissing life square on the mouth" greeted me from Cheryl's iPod. The room didn't smell like dead shrimp anymore and we were in a new town to explore. Blois, France, was home to French kings and queens, Leonardo da Vinci, and Joan of Arc. This was also reputed to be excellent cycling country and after being cooped up in the car for so long yesterday, we were longing to stretch our legs.

First stop was nearby Amboise for a visit to the Chateau du Clos Luce, the place when Leonardo da Vinci spent his last years with the support of King Francis I. Cheryl and I are fascinated by Leonardo with his progressive thoughts and inventions. This mansion and its gardens only whetted our appetite to learn more about this incredible man.

Arriving by mule in 1516, Leonardo brought with him three canvases of works-in-progress, which he finished painting in the studio and rose garden: The Mona Lisa, Sainte Anne, and Saint Jean Baptiste. He died in Amboise in 1519. The Parc showcases forty of his famous inventions in a setting of gardens, greenery, and waterfalls. A perfect spot to sit back and absorb the energy. So we did. For hours we basked in his inspiration. It was a glorious afternoon!

From the biking aspect, Blois was disappointing. In my mind's eye, we would be pedaling along the riverbank, wind in our hair, choosing which castles and chalets to visit with a picnic basket piled high with fresh French bread, fruits, pates, and cheese. Instead, we found narrow roads with no space for bicycles or even a view of the river. We were besieged by roaring trucks filled with all manner of smelly livestock and impossibly expensive bicycle rentals (that didn't even include a picnic hamper!). My dream of an afternoon of biking and hanging out under a tree with a book was shattered. We visited Chateau Chambord by car, but I was so disappointed about not being able to bike around the Loire Valley I stayed in the car for a nap while Cheryl toured the castle.

"You're not going to believe what I just ate!" she said proudly as she climbed back into the car.

I was just waking up from a long car nap and knowing Cheryl's usual reluctance to try new foods, wasn't as enthusiastic as I probably should have been. "Um, did you try a new cheese?" I offered.

"No, it wasn't cheese," she excitedly explained. "I stopped in one shop and was offered a piece of bread with a spread on it. The young man behind the counter told me it was very good. I was the only one in the shop and got the feeling he was glad just to have someone walk in. I'd told myself I would try new things on this trip, so didn't ask what it was. I popped it my mouth and it was actually quite good. While I still had it in my mouth, the guy told me it was lamb pate." She blanched as she spoke the words. Cheryl doesn't eat either lamb or pate. Never has and (before this trip) never would. "Now it was good, but you know I have this gag reflex that kicks in when I even think about eating something I normally wouldn't. I focused on chewing and swallowing as quickly as I could so I could avoid an unpleasant situation. Then I got out of there fast."

We stopped for dinner outside Blois, not willing to chance what the institutional menu might be in our prison home. Tin trays and splats of unidentified food brought back too many memories of college.

As the electric gate shut behind our car, we tried to figure out what sort of place this was we were staying. "The room is clean and we'll only be here for one more night," Cheryl placated and I agreed. At this point, the thought of packing up again to find another spot wasn't appealing. We were both beat and sleep seemed the best remedy.

By ten we were checked back into our room, not sure when "lights out" might happen. However, the prospect of waking the next day with no clean clothes wasn't one we wanted to face either. It was my turn to take laundry duty, so I headed back to the reception desk with my loaded bag and laundry soap sticking out of the top.

Our smiling friend from the previous night was at his post again. It was my turn to attempt communication. I pointed to the laundry bag and soap and asked where I could find the laundry. He just kept shaking his head. Over and over. He didn't understand what I was asking and I didn't know how to make it any more clear without the right words. I pointed again to my bag of smelly clothes and then the detergent. More shaking of the head.

I was getting more frustrated and grumpy by the second. At last, I saw a brochure on the counter for the hostel. I grabbed one and inside was a list of the amenities offered in French. Lavamatic was number three. I pointed to this on the pamphlet and the light bulb went off in his head. We were both smiling and pointing like two goofs, but I got the message it was downstairs. I needed to give him three euros, and then he produced tokens and a key. We nodded and grinned as the money and key were exchanged. He wrote down my room number and said something in emphatic French, pointing to the key. I assumed this meant to not lose the key to the laundry room, it was the only one they had.

Something I had not been aware of before our visit to France is many buildings have motion sensors on their hall and stairwell lights. It stays dark until someone walks through the sensor, triggering the lights to come on. But on this night, I spent ten minutes trying to balance my laundry load and find the stairwell light switch when, totally by accident, I activated the light and it came on. Whew! I didn't have to navigate those spooky stairs in the dark.

First level down and no sign of a laundry room. There was a nice foosball table, though.

Okay, down one more level to the basement. This time the stairwell lights came on just fine, but the basement was pitch-black. I felt along the cold concrete wall for the switch, my heart hammering with the fear of not knowing what my hand might touch next. I found it after only a few attempts, but by this time all I wanted was to get this laundry going and fast so I could get to bed. Once I got my bearings, I saw a ping pong table and five closed doors facing the common room.

Not one had anything written on it resembling "lavamatic" so I tried each door in turn. Mouth dry and fear trickling down my neck, I looked inside each one. I found dark, spooky closets, stacks of cleaning supplies, painting equipment, and finally the lavamatic.

Flipping the light switch, I got quite a surprise. The florescent bulb popped, hummed, and then sputtered menacingly. Only the vaguest sense of light was coming from the ceiling, bathing the empty room in a grey flickering hue. As hard as I tried not to think about it, the only thought running through my mind was the trailer for the movie *Hostel*. The flickering light bulb and serial killer with a huge knife. The entire audience thinking, "Why was she so stupid to go down there in the dark that time of night? It's a French basement lavamatic for goodness sake! They'll find her body stuffed in the dryer tomorrow!"

The upside was the washer and dryer were so small my whole body wouldn't have fit in it anyway. Downside, I had to start two loads to cover everything we'd dirtied up. I needed more coins for the machines. A trek back up the dark stairs to the reception desk to exchange more euros for tokens was in order. It was going to be a long night.

While waiting for the laundry to smell good again (it took one wash and two dries for each load, so I had plenty of time), I thought back to how innocently we'd jumped into this whole idea of living out of a backpack in a strange place almost every night. We'd left comfortable lives (and beds) in exchange for this chance to see things from a different perspective. My perspective now was listening to the hum of a dryer, sitting in a French basement, alone, in the dark.

I had to give Cheryl credit, though. She played down all the bad parts, knowing if I'd ever imagined myself sitting here now, I'd have balked at the idea of backpacking for thirteen weeks and tried to push for a long vacation somewhere on a beach instead.

Had it really just been a month since Cheryl proudly handed me a small package with strange stringy, yellow and black thing inside, saying "Look what I found!"? Gauging from her excitement level, I knew it must be something important. We'd made the trip to the Orlando camping superstore with our well-thought out lists in hand: flint, freeze-dried food, and batteries. But I didn't remember anything on the list looking quite like what she was putting into the shopping cart.

It was a simple clothesline. Double yellow cords entwined around each other. *Eliminates The Need For Clothespins* – the package claimed. What's a clothespin? My grandmother used those, but over the last twenty years or so they've been scarce around my house. Two hooks on the end because *It Will Hang Anywhere* – another package claim we never imagined we'd put to the test on car doors, window sills, bookcases, and rickety TV stands.

When trying to decide what to take when all your possessions will be stuffed in a backpack you're schlepping on your back, I hadn't put too much thought to the laundry issue.

"We'll be staying in hotels or hostels for the most part, right?" I pleaded. "In Europe they're pretty civilized spots, right? We'll have places with laundry facilities on the road, right?"

Cheryl was surprisingly non-committal on the laundry issue. She was focused on setting up a budget to allow us food, while I concentrated on how many pairs of pants and shirts and shoes I could bring along instead.

"I'm just planning for the what-if's," she said practically. As usual. "If we need to wash clothes on the road, then we should bring with us what we need."

I still wasn't entirely convinced, but started to look up references to "laundry" in the Rough Guides, around-the-world travel planners, and on-line forums. There wasn't much information out there. Sure, there were some vague references from travelers about washing out clothes in a gas station sink (Eww!) and to be sure to pack a sink plug (it was very important!).

So we came up with our own version of a "laundry sack". It was a compression bag we'd carry empty to fill up with dirties until we could get them washed. In it we'd put the clothesline, a plastic baggie filled with small containers of Woolite for our gentle items (yeah, right, like we wouldn't throw everything into one load anytime we could find a laundry!) and as an extra-special luxury item – a stack of lavender scented dryer sheets. Good-smelling things packed tight in a backpack are an indulgence you can't put a price on while traveling. And on the day before we left, I found the sink plug at the Dollar Store and threw it in for good measure. Just in case.

Laundry folded and warm, I returned the key and crept back to our room while Cheryl slept. That night I was soothed by the comforting smell of a freshly laundered t-shirt. Simple pleasures. Very nice.

8

*"All that is gold does not glitter,
Not all those who wander are lost"*

- J. R. R. Tolkien

Lyon and Marseille

It was a bit of a whirlwind driving through the entire countryside of France in three days on our way to the south. Our aim was to reach Nice to exchange our radio-free rental car and pick up the Open Road Peugeot we were buying for the rest of the trip. Unfortunately, because of the rush, the cities of Lyon and Marseille got skimped on in return. We learned a valuable lesson here, though. Spending only one night in a city just isn't enough. Our best memory of the glorious seaside city of Marseille is as the first place we dipped our toes in the chilly Mediterranean Sea. Brr!

In Lyon, the second largest city in France, we ached for steak. Asking at our hotel for a restaurant capable of easing our pain, we were directed to the Hippopotamus. From the name I worried what type of meat we might be eating, but was assured the cows we'd seen grazing on the roadsides were what the Hippo served. As it was something we'd both been craving and we felt a small reward was in order for consecutive days of eight to ten hours of driving, we ordered big.

Cheryl splurged on the chateaubriand and I ordered skewers of meat with a promise to help her finish her steak if it was too much to manage. At home, chateaubriand normally serves two and I was salivating in anticipation of sharing those juicy bites. Our meals came and were presented with a flourish capable of embarrassing most Paris waiters.

My plate was filled with a small assortment of sliced chicken, lamb, and vegetables. Certainly adequate, but not the luscious, dripping steak I'd imagined devouring. Cheryl's dish had nothing on it at all except a golf ball sized piece of animal protein. We stared at it in shock.

"Is this the chateaubriand?" we asked in unison, pointing at the bare plate as though it were an alien being.

"Yes, the chateaubriand," our eager waiter smiled, "the best!" He even kissed his fingertips for emphasis while he waited for Cheryl to take the first bite. There was barely more than a single bite, though she did deem it "the best thirty dollar steak I've had on the trip".

I shared my chicken with her and we left the restaurant with our heads hanging low and our wallets significantly lighter than when we'd arrived. As hard as I tried, I couldn't stop the dreams of Outback Steak House from torturing my mind all night.

While driving through the countryside of France, often as a treat we'd stop for a quick lunch beside the road. Our cooler filled with bread and cheese was far less expensive than finding a restaurant every day and watching the antics of fat, pollen covered honeybees cavorting in the sunflowers provided good fun. It was during these long drives when we came closer to defining the questions of our journey. Why were we doing this? What did we hope to accomplish? How had it changed us so far?

"My doctor told me if I didn't give up my high-stress job, it would continue to worsen my life," Cheryl confided. "High blood pressure, not being able to sleep, unhappiness. I put the stress on myself, but it consumed me. If I hadn't been able to step away from it, my health would have suffered."

My physical condition wasn't at stake, but my sanity was. I felt like a little hamster, waking up each morning to get on a wheel and run, run, run. Imagining a different life, but stuck in the habits and contentment of the one I had. I was afraid to move and I was at an impasse. I knew there was more out there to see and to be. This was my chance to experience life rather than simply reading about it in the books I loved. I wanted to write about the places we visited and the people we met to share with others. Surely we might be able to convince one or two others to step outside their own boundaries just a little. If we could do it, anyone could!

Nice

In a word – WOW! As we turned in for the drive along the Promenade des Anglais, Cheryl almost drove us off the road and into the incredible, jaw-dropping blue sea stretching out in front. Not that this would be such a horrible way to go – drowning in azure seas of the French Riviera with a background of craggy mountains, surrounded by tanned, fit, and mostly topless sunbathers. But alas, there was more for us to explore. She was able to keep the car on the road and still gape at the sapphire seas, so brilliantly beautiful it stunned the senses. The breezes from the Mediterranean quickly took away our car cramps and bathed us in the glow of a salty wish for an umbrella drink.

I fell head over heels in love with Nice the moment I smelled the sea. From the unimaginable beauty of the water to street names like Rue Dante and Boulevard Victor Hugo urging us deeper into the city to see her secret nooks and crannies. It was as if we'd stumbled upon a treasure chest of French delights.

Walking from the hotel to get a closer look at the sea and the sunbathers was like stepping into Wonderland. The streets shrank and became a village of intoxication. Smells of herbs de Province, fresh lavender, blooming flowers, soaps, perfumes, olive oil, wine casks, and rotisserie poulet assaulted our noses to the point of overload. I'd been nursing a cold the past few days and this sent my poor nose over the edge. One whiff of pepper and I started sneezing violently. Not a pretty picture when mounds of fresh spices are within inches of the narrow, crowded walkways. Everywhere my nose tried to find breathing room, there was more – spice, sweet, fishy, flowery, curious, and foreign. It was a feast for the senses, even if your nose is determined to inflict public embarrassment.

On the tapering, fragrant roads, I drove Cheryl crazy taking pictures of everything. "Look!" I shouted after her. "Did you know there were so many different types of salt? Black salt, red salt from Hawaii, fresh sea salt from the Mediterranean…did you imagine?" As I snapped more pictures, Cheryl kept walking, trying to lose me in the crowd.

I finally found her again at a bend in the street watching curiously as a man hacked on a pig. It was a whole pig – dead I assumed – as its entire carcass was filled with meats, stuffing, and spices. The server would chop off a piece with his cleaver and hand it to a waiting customer who happily munched on his prize while walking down the boulevard. It was our first introduction to a porchetta and I was appalled.

Not getting out much back home, I'd never seen or heard of the practice of gutting, de-boning, and spit roasting a pig; then serving him all opened up and exposed like that. It seemed awfully barbaric, though my appetite for pancetta wasn't dampened a bit.

Taking a "day off" while traveling seems a little like an oxymoron, but we quickly found it becomes entirely necessary to retain one's good nature about the trials of travel. Our day was spent on the beach in Nice, relaxing under an umbrella and splurging on the expense of two chaise lounges. I guess it wasn't too much of a splurge as there was no way in hell either of us was going to lie all day on the rocks passing for beach sand here.

"Where's the sand?" I asked as we walked along the promenade. I had our beach equipment in tow: Cheryl's iPod, my books and journals, towels, and sunscreen – though from the leathery looks of most bathers, sunscreen must be a priceless commodity here.

"No sand. It's just rocks," Cheryl said squinting at the sun. "All those people are lying directly on the rocks."

"Ouch. They must be tough people." We quickly agreed we were not tough people and it would be okay to split the twelve euros cost for two lounges, a table, and an umbrella.

Shades of blue shifted as the sun moved over us. The harbor sky became filled with approaching planes, huge animals dodging their way through brave-souled parasailers. On the beach, we picked through rocks like we would seashells back home; a pretty pink one here, another smooth one spreading warmth to my hand. Small souvenirs to take back home from the Cote l' Azure and promptly forget. Though Nice is one place I don't think we'll ever forget – here the sun warms, the wines soothe, and the herbs and perfumes quench our thirst for sensory amusement.

The Mediterranean Sea captivated us so much, that back in the room, Cheryl began a quest to get us out there on it. Typing on the computer with the ease of someone who's by now accessed thousands of travel web sites, she quickly came up with an idea.

"There are a couple of options to get us on the water. We could sign up to work as crew for one of the sailboats in the harbor. There are some ads on-line. They are looking for people to cook, clean, and help sail the boat. It would be an experience we'd never forget."

"Sounds interesting. But you said there was another option?" Although definitely exciting, the idea of being trapped on a small boat with strangers on the fickle sea wasn't exactly winning me over.

"Then how would you feel about a Mediterranean cruise?"

Hmm, now I'd be trapped on a big boat with strangers. But here the perks were much better. "I like cruises. All the food you can eat. Parties on deck. Deck chairs and Jacuzzis. Midnight buffets and ice cream all day – sign me up!"

"I found one leaving from Rome in a week. It's a last minute deal, so for $499 we'd spend seven days cruising to Sicily, around the Greek Islands – Mykonos, Patmos, Santorini, and then Izmir, Turkey. It's almost less expensive than staying in hotels and all our food and transportation is included. Would this be something you'd like to do?"

Happy thoughts were rushing through my mind at warp speed – bacon, crunchy ice, rum drinks with umbrellas, flaming desserts, four-course dinners. Whoa! "What about the formal dress code?" I wept. "Don't cruises require you to dress up every night for dinner?"

Being banished from the luscious dining room was an unimaginable plight. Yet, not one item in our backpack wardrobe was formal in character. Zip-off pants and flip flops wouldn't make the cut for entrance into the land of cruise ship haute cuisine. I was almost in tears. So close to bacon, so close!

"We'll just have to pick up some dress clothes here in Nice. There are so many shops here, I'm sure we'll be able to find something to get us through."

So off we went. To a chaotic morning of pointing, trying on, shaking heads, figuring out comparable sizes in French, and finally sagging with exhaustion at the nearby gelato stand.

French shoes for me were out of the question. I can barely walk without falling in bare feet, so the thought of strapping on three-inch spiked heels and walking on a rolling ship deck brought tremors and chills. My dusty Keens would have to do.

"Maybe if I come to the dinner table early and hide my feet, so no one will see my shoes?"

Cheryl tried to assure me no one would care, but from a peek on the cruise web site for formal dress nights; my ratty shoes would most definitely be noticed. I didn't let it worry me too much, though. I let my dreams of unlimited servings of crispy bacon override my shame.

We finished our delightfully sticky lunchtime gelatos sitting on one of the many fountains in Nice. I was still busy thinking thoughts of tanned bartenders serving my every whim from a deck chair; when a family came up to the fountain and started splashing water on their faces.

"Have you noticed how different it is here?" Cheryl observed. "Fountains are everywhere. Some people fill their water bottles, others drink directly from it with their hands, and some are even using them to wash up after they eat lunch. The water is so clean, clear, and cool. In America, you wouldn't even consider doing any of these things. Matter of fact, you would be probably looked down on or even asked by police to move on. These fountains seem to be for public use."

It *was* a different concept. We watched as people washed their hands, face, and finished up with a general splash over their bodies. Our hands were sticky from the gelato, so we joined in as well – fountain bathing in Nice!

Picking up our Open Road car in the Nice airport provided one of the more hilarious misadventures of the trip. Though only after the fact! The plan was simple. Cheryl would drop me and all our bags at the airport Arrivals hall, while she returned the rental car. We'd meet at the Peugeot Open Road booth inside the airport. Simple enough, right?

I jumped out of the car and went in search of one of those handy carts to schlep stuff around the airport. When I came back with the cart, Cheryl and the car were gone. She'd been shooed away by the police!

I'm pushing my empty little cart around for about ten minutes trying to figure out where she might be – then she appears. She's had to park under the airport as there was no curbside loading zone. Off we go to find the car and load the luggage.

I think it was my bright idea to strap the two backpacks together on the cart. Otherwise, their width wouldn't fit through the narrow airport door – or so I tell myself now. Total backpack poundage was close to fifty-five pounds. We'd also accumulated a few other things as well. Three large assorted bags of groceries and limoncello, and both our day bags perched on top. It was quite a full little cart.

Cheryl went to return the car and off I trundled with my load through the airport. I looked like the world's most prosperous bag lady as I could barely see over the mountain of packs. I found the lift quickly – elevators are called lifts here – and set out for Floor Zero from Floor Two. Unfortunately, the lift only went as far as Floor One. To get to the next floor required navigation through a series of moving walkways and escalators that only grudgingly accepted the creaking cart I was shoving through.

The straps from the packs kept getting caught up in the wheels, so every few feet I would stop, back up to unwind the mess, then head on again. I was almost there – just one more moving walkway and I could see the Open Road kiosk – way down at the bottom. I didn't realize it at the time, but the walkway angle steeped precipitously downward.

In seconds, the entire load tipped forward and fell off the cart. The straps, tangled in the cart wheels moments before, now became snarled in the stairs of the moving walkway. The whole walkway was completely blocked with no chance of clearing soon. Normally, this wouldn't be so bad. But the large group of touring Germans stuck behind me wasn't the least bit happy about being delayed for their flight by a mass of knotted backpacks and a rolling tin of tuna fish escaping from one of the grocery bags.

Soon – much too soon in my state of humiliation, we reached the end of the footway. We were deposited on Floor Zero, but there was no place for any of us to go. The thumping and grinding sound the moving walkway made as it tried to eat our bags still haunts me to this day. The pointed glares from the trapped Germans mobilized my mortified body to hop over the hurdle and start tugging frantically from the other side. Considerable yanking did the trick and after what seemed like days, the pile moved – right on top of me.

I sat buried under the tangled mess, while the impatient tour group stepped around me and went on their way without a word. "I'm fine," I muttered after them, silently wishing for each piece of their luggage to get lost before the return trip.

Thanks to a healthy boost of adrenaline, I got the entire jumble loaded back onto the cart. Except for the tin of tuna – I never did find it.

"Where have you been?" Cheryl asked when I caught up with her a few minutes later. "You look all sweaty. You won't believe how hard it was finding where to drop off the rental car. I had to drive around and around."

I rolled my eyes and hoped she wouldn't notice the ripped straps or the hunk of nylon chewed out of one of the packs.

It's all worth it though, as we drive out of Nice with our shiny, still-smells-like-new-car Peugeot. There are only four kilometers on the odometer! We head for the sights of Italy, riding along the coastal roads. Mountains and terraced hills on one side and the marvelous, cerulean Mediterranean Sea on the other. And the very best part? We have a radio! Yippee!

9

"I dislike feeling at home when I am abroad"

- George Bernard Shaw

Grosseto

I woke up in a tent! Not a caravan or RV, but an actual canvas tent. How on earth did we sink this low?

"But I told you I'd made reservations for us to stay at a campground. Where did you think we'd be sleeping?" Cheryl's voice rose to be heard over the wild cacophony of pre-dawn-rising cicadas.

I shouted back, "I heard you mention a camping resort. A resort usually means an attached bathroom and cute little kitchenette. And why on earth are those bugs creating such a racket? It's only six AM."

Cheryl groaned and rolled over on her cot. I sat up, tried to stand and get dressed in the four inch space separating our cots. "I'm going to find the bathroom."

"'Kay," she mumbled and went right back to sleep. I couldn't blame her. We had driven for over ten hours yesterday, covering the south of France to the middle of Italy all in one day. Our only stop had been to visit Pisa – as in The Leaning Tower Of – or in Italian, La Torre di Pisa.

While driving the beautiful roads of Tuscany, I noticed on the map the town of Pisa wasn't far from the highway. Because I'm always on the lookout for the perfect Pisa picture, we stopped to take a look. There it was – the Campanile or bell tower – leaning in all its glory. As with most things I've only seen before in pictures, the size was a little disappointing. I thought it would be bigger.

The Campo Santo cemetery was of almost as much interest as the Tower everyone flocks to see. Claimed to be the most beautiful in the world, it was built around a shipload of sacred soil brought over in the twelfth century during the Fourth Crusade from the site of Golgotha.

The Tower, Duomo cathedral, Baptistry, and Campo Santo make up what's known as the Piazza dei Miracoli or Square of Miracles. What seemed miraculous now was the number of people behaving like goofballs trying to get a picture either pretending to prop up the Tower or carry it in the palm of their hand. It was insane. Children in strollers would have daddy placing their palm in just the right spot while mommy giggled and took the shot. Teens with a nonchalant slouch would pretend to be holding it up with their weight. Even the older set was getting into the act, as old ladies in colorful hats posed tipping forward with both hands stretched out in front. I stood shaking my head in embarrassment for them.

After we took our own "holding up the Tower" photos, we piled back into the car and headed south. Our destination was Marina di Grosseto for the Le Marze Camping Village Resort. Somewhere in passing I'd heard the word "resort" and kind of missed the "camping" part. Described on-line as "situated on a beautiful stretch of the Tyrrhenian coast on a sandy beach in the Maremma National Park", it sounded delightful.

Driving directions were as clear as a muddy stream – like most we followed on this trip. *On SS-1 E 80 Aurelia, take exit Follonica Nord, drive through Follonica on the SP152 and follow Marina di Grosseto on the SP158 until km300+200.* Huh?

The word travel stems from the French word travail – to work hard or labor. Considering how often we got lost and the labor involved with getting us back on track, I'd say this was a fair definition of the word.

Having our own car meant we weren't tied to specific schedules, but it didn't guarantee we wouldn't spend hours upon hours trying to find where we were on the map and where we wanted to be.

"Argh!" Cheryl thumped the steering wheel in frustration. "This is driving me crazy. Street signs are non-existent and the numbers marked change from one side of a road to another. To our right the road is called SP152, but on the other side it's called SP12!"

By now it was well past our typical bedtime and we hadn't seen anything looking like an SP158. The map wasn't helpful. It didn't even have SP158 listed as an option. We drove past numerous dark Italian villages, wondering if we'd ever find a place to lay our heads for the night.

By ten, we were so tired the idea of simply pulling off the road and sleeping for a few hours in the car became an alternative. Only the idea of a groggy midnight rout by Italian carabinieri in shiny boots kept us driving.

By some miracle we passed a sign – Marina di Grosseto – and turned into tight Italian streets. We were so happy to have finally discovered at least one landmark, it didn't matter that it was another half-hour before we stumbled on the Le Marze Resort. I was so pleased we found someone still awake enough to check us in, it didn't fully register we were sleeping in a tent.

This being a campground with people on holiday, we were pleasantly surprised to find everyone awake and still going strong when we unpacked. The disco was blaring on one side of the resort and the teen dance night was in full swing just a short distance from our beds. Rather than being aggravated, we were amazingly revived. There was life outside a stuffy car and we'd found it here!

"I'm hungry," Cheryl said.

I was exhausted from the intensive concentration required by hours of navigation, but my stomach was wide awake and grumbling. "Yeah, me too. Let's go see what we can find!"

Imagine our disappointment when we entered the Pizza Pub to find them shutting the doors for the night. Lingering smells of roasted garlic still hung in the air, our mouths watering with futile anticipation.

"Chiuso? Are you closed?" We tapped feebly at the door.

The young waitress inside looked as weary as we felt. She'd been waiting on hordes of hungry campers all day and was probably ready to take off her flour-coated apron and go join the dancers on the entertainment stage. As we turned to slink back to the tent to dig out some stale crackers from the car, a young man with a thousand watt smile, stacking a mountain of pizza boxes, said something to her in Italian and she nodded for us to come in.

It must have been the awful road-weary vibe we were giving off, because our hero motioned us beside him at the pizza oven and asked what would make us happy.

"I love the Italians," I said with my mouth full of ham and mushrooms, while artichokes and black olives, tucked in miles of gooey cheese, streamed down my chin.

This is the best pizza I've ever put into my mouth," Cheryl swooned.

Smiling at the thought of the wonderful pizza we'd inhaled the night before; my quest to find the WC this morning became a bit more bearable. It was only a short walk from our tent, but somehow I got turned around and managed to get hopelessly lost on my way back. Stumbling over tree roots and holding my ears to avoid the torrent of sound the cicadas were producing in the branches above me, I staggered through the woods. Only the smell of cooking bacon coming from a large motor home nearby gave me bearings I needed to find my way back to our humble green tent.

Reading in the tent was impossible. I'm not sure how Cheryl was sleeping through all the racket the cicadas were creating. I'd been to football games quieter than these guys.

Stomach growling from the wafting drifts of breakfasty smells invading our tent; I went in search of breakfast. I imagined eggs and ham with a side of home fries piled high on a plate. What I got was a *paste* – sugar coated dough filled with the creamiest of custards – it was yummy, but I wanted bacon.

I sat stuffing my face with goo, lamenting how much I craved protein. France had been a Mecca of culinary delights, but I'd consumed too many assorted pizzas, tagliatelles, and spaghetti bolognaise (heavy on the spag, light on the bol) for my waistline to stand a chance. So in defiance, I ordered another sweet paste. It was delicious.

"I thought this campground was on the beach," Cheryl said as she finally came out to greet the day.

"Thought so, too. But I checked the brochure map, because that's what I do best, and the beach is across the street. They have sun-loungers for rent. We can practice for the cruise!"

"Sounds like a plan," she said. "Is that bacon I smell? Let's order a big breakfast." See? I wasn't the only one.

A day spent on the latte-colored beaches of the Tyrrhenian coast was exactly what we needed, even without bacon. It was paradise. Much warmer than those of the Mediterranean in Nice, the silky soft waters left you wondering what other sun-kissed beaches they has recently caressed.

Kite boarders fill the sky with color diversion in case one could tire of gazing at the beautiful blue. Their antics made me want to try. Where else can you combine the love of being on the water with flying? Fortunately for my insurance premiums, lessons weren't offered that day.

We did enjoy the sun loungers, but I was enamored with the sand. Real sand. Not like the rocks in Nice. It was as brown as toasted caramel. Watching the children laugh in glee as they ran their fingers through the warm brown sugar, covering themselves from head to toe with handfuls before chirping and running headlong into the gentle surf. It was pure entertainment. A parade of diminutive naked bodies rushed by in wholesome innocence, giggling as they tumbled over each other. White bottoms dot bright beach towels and smiles abound.

We finished off the day at the Beach Bar, where they serve a large glass of Italian rum for two euros – Woo Hoo! Elvis is singing *All Shook Up* and nearby children smell sweet, fresh from the sea, or maybe it's the ice cream dripping from their chins? Cheryl is smiling from ear to ear and my only wish at this moment is to watch the sun set over the Mediterranean Sea for the first time.

Leaving the Le Marze Camping Resort was a lot harder than I would have believed. I'd grown accustomed to the pub, pizza kitchen, piano bar, supermarket, and bazaar available to us. It wasn't like any campground I'd ever visited before and throwing in the incredible beach – I didn't want to leave.

"Maybe we should come back here after the cruise?" I asked. My senses were soothed here and I knew if I pushed a little harder we could probably upgrade from tent to camper next time around.

To Cheryl, it must have felt like having me along was akin to babysitting a small child. I never seemed to be happy. "We'll be in Rome after the cruise, but I'm sure we can come back if we have the time," she offered kindly.

The Mediterranean cruise left in four days, so our next destination needed to be within easy driving distance of the port of Civitavecchia, near Rome. Finding a place was easier than pronouncing the name. We got on the Internet, consulted a map of Italy, and found what appeared to be a charming little town called Viterbo just a few hours south. In twenty minutes, Cheryl finalized reservations for us to stay at a place called the Hotel Mini Palace and had printed detailed directions on how to get there the next day. We could enjoy the beach at Le Marze one more day.

Viterbo

It was like trading in our tent for the Taj Mahal!

Turns out Viterbo was only a two hour drive from Grosseto and wonder of all wonders – we found the hotel on the very first try. The signs and directions helped a bunch. When we checked into the Hotel Mini Palace our jaws dropped. For about forty euros a night, we got a room at the equivalent of the Four Seasons of Viterbo. The décor was sumptuous dark forest greens, thick carpets, heavy woods, and a bed with pillows capable of swallowing a person whole. We'd landed in another world from the sweaty, noisy tent occupied the night before. And here we didn't have to share a bathroom with other sandy campers.

The charm of Viterbo went much further than the hotel. Huge medieval city walls called us to explore even though it was stifling hot outside. We picked up a map from the front desk, took a deep breath to brace against the two PM heat, and headed out – right into the middle of siesta. This was a new concept for us. Everything in the city closes shop from one PM until four-thirty. Everything.

It was as though we'd stumbled upon an ancient ghost town. The labyrinth of cobblestone streets were spookily quiet and not even the dogs roamed around in the heat. This wasn't the best time to be starving, but I was. Breakfast had been many hours before and not nearly as satisfying as I'd imagined a huge Italian lunch in Viterbo to be. We passed quaint restaurants that teased with delightful menus displayed outside, but doors were tightly shut and not a soul stirred inside.

Romanesque churches dating back to the ninth century enticed us with cool stones and quiet pews to linger inside, but the horrendous rumbling sounds from my stomach were starting to embarrass Cheryl. I needed to find food fast. Saying a small prayer to the patron saint of afternoon snacks, we ventured out again.

It was a miracle! Turning a corner from one of the musical fountains, we found a small café with actual people inside. There were only three tiny tables to sit, but a long line in front of the bar. Waiting our turn, we noticed no one else was eating. Instead, everyone ordered a large glass of one of the spirits behind the bar. With glass in hand, they downed the contents in one or two solid gulps, put the glass back on the counter, and walked back outside.

"Do you serve food?" I asked cautiously in English. Cautiously, because I thought I'd break down in tears if she said no, and I wasn't sure if English was spoken in such a tiny town.

Sylvia greeted us with a big smile. "Ah, yes we do. I do, anyway. Welcome. I can practice my English with you." It was a mutually beneficial meeting. We got to taste her version of what she called pizza, but really was two slices of salty, crunchy bread with prosciutto and cheese inside. Whether one called it pizza or a toasted ham and cheese sandwich was irrelevant. It was simply delicious. Sylvia had just returned home from a two year visit to England and was eager to talk when she could find a spare second.

Taking one of the empty tables, we watched as a steady stream of patrons came in, each ordering something in a large glass from the bar and tossing it back, wiping their chins on the back of their hands and going back out.

It was the uniformed postman on his motorbike who pushed me over the edge. As he swigged his drink, laughingly paid a few coins, left the bar and hopped back on his bike to continue his deliveries; Sylvia came over to ease the look of surprise on my face. "This is the end of siesta time. After everyone has gone home for a big lunch with their families and maybe a short nap, it's time for a digestive." She explained limoncello, jagermeister, amaretto, and even whiskey were her big sellers.

"Then they go back to work?" I asked, incredulous. Closing for lunch, naptime, and having permission to drink before going back to work – these were all appealing to me. This European tradition was something I could get used to, I just had to be careful not to get run over by the happy postman after he'd enjoyed his digestive.

After learning the customs of Italian siesta, it was time to venture into more dangerous territories. At the hotel front desk, we asked for a dinner recommendation and were told of a place in the medieval section of town serving excellent food. Sylvia's pizza kept our appetites in check until we dared go back out to roam the streets.

Ancient city gates of lava stone built in the eleventh and twelfth centuries and rising over thirty feet high welcomed us back. I was fascinated by this well-preserved city, once the residence of the popes. The Palazzo dei Papi or Papal Palace is an elegant building and one of the most famous monuments of the town. Built between 1255 and 1267, this grand structure is characterized by its loggia (balcony) with massive, but intricate arches.

It is a classic city in the largest sense. The homes cut into stone side-by-side; open windows so close the neighbors have no doubt what the latest family discord was all about in all its detail. Did they learn not to listen?

Laundry is hung outside with no shame for all to see. When Sylvia washes her new nightie for the first time, I'm sure the whole village is envious.

What I fell in love with most in this town were the lions. There are statues of lions, lions painted on frescos, doorknockers with the faces of lions; some serene, some fierce. Asking around about the prevalence of so many lions, we were told the lion represents Hercules, one of the mythological founders of Viterbo.

"Are you taking another picture of a doorknob?" Cheryl asked as we explored more of the Quarter of Saint Pellegrino.

"These lions are so beautiful. And they're working doorknockers. I have an idea! I think I'll make a coffee table book called Knockers of Italy. Think it would sell?"

Cheryl just rolled her eyes and kept on walking. "The restaurant should be just down the next street," she said, disappearing around the corner while I worked on getting perfect composition for my fifty-third doorknocker picture of the day.

Our first hint of trouble should have been when we were seated by the charming Italian waiter and given our menus written entirely in the native language. This had happened a few times before, but we were always able to muddle through to some extent. No worries yet. We exchanged small pleasantries of hello and good evening with him in Italian – the absolute limit of our Italian language knowledge – then politely asked if there was a menu with English subtitles. A bewildered look greeted our question and our worst fear was realized – not only did he speak no English, there was no one else working there who did either. The menu was an extensive treasure chest of what we could only imagine was not-to-miss gastronomic delights.

"Can you see anything that looks familiar?" I asked, pausing to thumb through our completely useless Italian-to-English translator.

"Nothing. I can usually pick out spaghetti or prosciutto or something. Nothing looks recognizable. And I really don't want to order something like frog cheeks. As daring as I'm trying to be with my food choices, I don't think I'd enjoy those at all."

I had to agree. An Italian meal is a work of art served in three to five courses. Could we take a chance our fingers would blindly point to the right thing for every course? We were in a severe dining dilemma.

"Using this phrasebook we have I can say 'I have nothing to declare' or 'Could you prepare my meal without beef stock', but I can't order anything on this menu," I fumed.

"Everyone here is speaking Italian," Cheryl observed. "At the next table over is a man and his daughter, they've finished eating so I wonder if it would be rude to ask if they could help us?"

Being the brave traveler she is, Cheryl leaned over at a small lull in their perfect Italian conversation. "Excuse me, I don't mean to interrupt your dinner, but you wouldn't happen to speak a bit of English, would you?"

The booming laugh was answer enough, but the "Why, of course I do! I'm from New Mexico!" had us grinning from ear to ear. He was in Viterbo as Associate Conductor for the visiting New Mexico Symphony Orchestra performing all week. "What can I do to help?" he asked.

"Perhaps a recommendation for dinner, as we're not as knowledgeable about reading Italian as we should be and our phrasebook isn't very helpful."

Not only did he provide several wonderful recommendations, he even ordered our courses and dessert in Italian for the relieved waiter. The meal was incredible! I enjoyed a beefsteak smothered in an apple cream sauce so fantastic I practically licked the plate.

When we returned to our room that evening, we were determined this wouldn't happen again while we were in Italy. One of our basic traveling tenants abroad is to never assume or even hope people always spoke English. We are visiting their country and it's our responsibility to be knowledgeable enough with the language to get by. This ensures we learn something in the process and seems a better way to visit a country.

If the last meal was any indication, we knew we'd be doing lots more eating in Italy. So we got to work. It was time to throw out the hopeless phrasebook and design our own real life "cheat sheet".

"What do you absolutely want to avoid eating?" Cheryl asked, pen poised and Internet humming beside her.

"I'm not a big fan of veal or rabbit."

"Okay, those would be scaloppini and coniglio. What about snails?"

"Eww. Yes, please put snails on the 'do not eat list'."

When finished, we'd put together a fairly comprehensive page of things we wouldn't be caught dead putting into our mouth: brains (cervello), pigeon (piccione), or frog (ranocchio).

The next time we sat down to eat, we confidently ordered the primi, secundi, dessert, and even a bottle of excellent wine with our "cheat sheet" tucked inside the menu. We even ran into our conductor friend again the next day.

"Do you ladies need any help reading the menu here?" He asked with a grin.

"Tonight we have it under control, but thank you so much for saving us last night," Cheryl said gratefully.

The frutti de mare was the best I've ever eaten. The pride taken in not ordering the braised animelle (sweetbreads) instead was priceless.

10

"It may be that the satisfaction I need depends on my going away, so that when I've gone and come back, I'll find it at home."

- Rumi

Civitavecchia, Rome

From childhood I've always been fascinated by mythology. As soon as I could reach the books on the shelves I pulled down Bullfinch's Mythology and Age of Fable. The pictures of Hera and Zeus, Diana, and the boy who burned up in the sun as he tried to fly were sometimes frightening, but they told incredible tales of quests for gold, glory, or a fleece. These were my childhood heroes and today we're cruising through the very waters where these stories originated. Their voices are on the waves and under the deepest parts of this blue sea. Our itinerary for the trip includes Catania in Sicily, Patmos and Mykonos to sample Greek island life, Izmir, Turkey to explore Ephesus and the home of the Virgin Mary, then back to Rome. I couldn't be much happier.

"Do you want to board the ship early?" Cheryl asked. "We won't leave until five, but we can check out the boat early and maybe even grab lunch on board."

Lunch! There is was. Seafood salad, green salad, green beans with tuna, lasagna, pizza, potato and onion soufflé, ice cream…I ate like I hadn't eaten in six months. All at once and some of it twice!

"We can't do this every day," I said with my mouth stuffed full of lasagna. "We'll gain twenty pounds."

"You're right. They have an exercise room and spa here. Let's take advantage of it. We should use their personal trainer to keep us on track."

I wasn't totally on board with the whole exercise-on-the-boat routine until she mentioned the magic word – bacon. "Exercise has its own reward. If we work out, you can eat all the bacon you want and not feel guilty about it."

The next morning (after a rousing forty minute pounding on the Stairmaster), I stood in the buffet line with an angel on my shoulder beaming and pointing to the one thing I'd been craving for over two months. Crispy, crunchy, perfectly cooked bacon. Ahh! I savored each slice as though I'd never get another. My leg muscles twinged slightly, but my stomach felt great. This was going to be one fun cruise.

Having all announcements on board in Italian sometimes became a little confusing. "Did the loudspeaker just say stromboli?" I asked from the deck. "I think I heard stromboli. It must mean they're serving stromboli somewhere on board. I should go look."

My venture toward the food deck (my favorite place) brought me through throngs on camera-wielding people on deck, all straining to see something far off in the distance.

"What's out there?" I asked a man with a Boston Red Sox hat and a massive camera.

"Stromboli," he said and continued snapping. Great, I had heard correctly.

Looking around the crowded deck, I concluded that he must have already eaten. There was no stromboli anywhere in sight. Not even a whiff of garlic in the air. Stomach growling and impatient to find the feast, I asked another family where I might find the stromboli.

"There," she pointed out to sea. "We're sailing toward it. It's an erupting volcano." She must have noticed my bewildered look because she kept on explaining, "See, the island just over there. That's Stromboli."

Who knew? And I'd had my heart set on pepperoni. It was hard to be too disappointed at missing food, though, when the sight was so amazing. As we came close to the island, you could see lava and steam flows coming from its top. Nature's energy expenditures were massive here. Ducking back onto the food deck, I enjoyed a slice of Parma pizza while snapping my own pictures of my new favorite Stromboli.

Catania, Sicily

First cruise stop – Catania. Founded in 729 B.C. as one of the first Greek colonies in Sicily, this island is the home to Mt. Etna. This gave us two active volcanoes in one day! My volcano fix will be good for a few more months.

Portside, Catania wasn't much to write home about. Container ships and cargo belts led the way to Timberland, Wrangler, and Coin shops along the main pedestrian streets. The touristy stuff got boring pretty quick, so we ducked into a side street to watch a wedding in progress. Massive sculptures on the cathedral steps were held aloft by sparkling balloons. The bride appeared in the doorway to whoops from family and friends.

On the way back to the ship, we came upon three older Sicilian women in housedresses sitting on a back stoop with laundry baskets at their feet. As we passed by, all three waved and gave us huge toothless smiles of welcome.

Back on the ship, we were treated to a spectacular view of Mt. Etna in the sunset. With everyone else in port, we found a quiet spot on the back of the ship to sip a carafe of wine and watch as the sky absorbed the mountain in relief.

Toasting to friendship. To having this opportunity of time and space to write and absorb. To living a dream of seeing the world. To possibly prompt others with the same urge tugging at their own subconscious, just far enough out of the skin to be an annoying splinter. So many toasts we had to order another carafe.

The sea breeze blew cool over our sun-toasted skin, voices in the background a cacophony of languages – French, Italian, German, and English; all blending together with the salty smell of Sicily. We're about two months into the trip with five more weeks left. A friend recently asked, "So what does it feel like never to have to go home from vacation?" Because neither of us owns a home to go back to right now, it feels pretty good. When we leave this cruise and go on to the next place; we'll stop only to do laundry and pick up the Internet messages we've missed while wandering the Aegean Sea.

Small twinges of guilt nagged us about laying down our backpacks for the cool comfort of a cruise ship. But the price was right and it gave us a chance to see places we wouldn't have been able to visit on our budget. Being on a cruise ship isn't a bad way to live, especially because they have so much bacon here.

"Cheryl, I'll die of embarrassment if they ask us to leave," I whispered on the way to dinner the first night.

"You look fine. Don't worry; no one will notice your shoes."

"Easy for you to say, you found dress shoes in Nice. All I have are my Keens." I looked around furtively for a bruising bouncer with an eye for inappropriate footwear. Seeing a clear path to a table, I quickly slid my legs under the tablecloth and breathed a sigh of relief. As long as I didn't have to get up during dinner, I could enjoy this feast.

We explained to the others sharing our table our clothing predicament and to expect only a collage of beige travel clothes, even on the "dress-up" nights. To my relief, they couldn't have cared less. After a day of exploring on our own, it was great fun to catch up with everyone and what they had discovered on the island excursions. It was also nice to have some else to talk to beside ourselves!

Patmos, Greece

"Six AM? The tender leaves at six in the morning? I thought this was supposed to be a relaxing cruise," I muttered groggily as we grabbed our daypacks and followed the lines of other sleepy cruisers to the bobbing boats waiting to take us to the island of Patmos.

On my best day I'm not the world's most coordinated person – maybe not even in the top sixty percent – but throw in half-asleep, pitching waves, and a very wide jump required to throw oneself into the tender and there's a recipe for maritime disaster. Luckily the crew had strong arms. When I catapulted myself into the boat with momentum threatening to carry me right through to the sea on the other side, I was clothes-lined with authority and shown my seat at the rear. Cheryl climbed in easily.

"So what's in Patmos?" I asked, pulling out the obligatory Greek Islands guidebook we'd been marking up for days. I hadn't had my bacon or coffee yet, so the details were a bit blurry.

"A special place. They call this the Holy Island of the Aegean. The Monastery of St. John is here and so is the cave where John, as an exiled disciple of Jesus

Christ, is said to have written the Book of Revelation from a dream from God," Cheryl read.

Trying to get in the right frame of mind to visit such a holy place was easier than I expected. The sunrise over the dusky blue waters revealed cliffs dotted with an abundance of whitewashed dwellings. As we docked and found our way on shore in Hora, a nun in black habit and slow steps of age climbed the steep entrance of a nearby church, a grey tabby following on her heels.

"Is this the monastery?" We asked a group of waiting cab drivers. They laughed. "Is it close by?" They chuckled again.

A tall, weather-worn Greek with the obligatory fishing cap extended his hand and pointed up. "The monastery is up there. I take you."

I could see nothing but sharp, exposed cliffs looking up and it had been dark as we came ashore. Trusting this man to know where his island's monastery was located, we negotiated a seven euros price for the trip. Off we went.

"Oh my God!" I screamed as we took swerve after swerve over steep switchbacks, passing enormous tour buses, and looking down at what appeared to be a most painful fall back down into the sea. It was a white-knuckled ride I was only happy to see finished.

"Should I wait for you?" Our driver asked with a maniacal grin on his face.

"S'okay," I answered shakily. "We'll walk down." It had to be safer than trusting our speed demon over those narrow roads playing chicken with a bus.

A short walk up more steepness and we were at the Monastery of St. John the Divine. The views from the top were breathtaking. Our ship seemed so small in the distance and the hum of more buses straining up the hills motivated us to hurry inside before the crowds arrived.

"You'll need to wear these," a soft-spoken monk of the Patmian Brotherhood told us as we entered. "These" were holy skirts to pull on over our clothes to cover our legs. Denim isn't my favorite material and the elastic waist wasn't the most flattering fashion statement. In fact, I looked even lumpier than usual. But I sucked it up. We were in God's house and we'd follow the customs. Men in shorts were required to pull on a pair of elastic trousers as well, so all visitors looked properly reverent, if not a bit out-of-date.

"It's so beautiful," Cheryl whispered. Founded in 1088, this magnificent structure sits atop the island; housing invaluable paintings, manuscripts, and holy vestments. The ornate carvings of gold, intricate mosaics, and icons of St. John adorn the monastery in every nook and cranny.

"It's not what I expected. I thought a small Greek island like this would have a simple monastery. Austere, not with the beauty and wealth so obvious here. It's amazing."

We learned the reason for the ten separate chapels within the monastery. "The Orthodox Church doesn't allow celebrating Mass at the same Chancel table more than once a day," the guide explained.

The Treasury (or Library) wasn't available for us to explore. But just hearing about the wealth of history in the thirty-three pages of a sixth century manuscript of St Mark's Gospel and an eighth century manuscript of the Book of Job had me breaking out in goose bumps yet again.

When we finally were able to drag ourselves away, it was time to return our skirts and start the downhill journey to the Holy Cave of the Apocalypse.

"I think the holy skirt gave me a rash," I complained. "I'm all itchy now."

Cheryl rolled her eyes and tried to find the right path through the forest. "It's the road pilgrims take from Hora all the way up to the Monastery. The Cave should be just down the hill."

Being especially thankful we were taking the steep path down rather than up, I plodded along and tried not to think about my itchy legs.

"There it is. John's cave." Cheryl whispered reverently. Quiet murmurs of prayerful pilgrims greeted our ears and a worshipful calm pervaded the small space. The coolness inside was such a welcome relief from the nagging heat of Patmos.

Reading the inscription over the door brought another round of goose bumps I couldn't blame on the cool air: *As dreadful as this place is it is nevertheless the house of God and this is the Gate of Heaven.*

"In the Greek world," our guide explained, "This place is called the Holy Cave of the Apocalypse. John, beloved disciple of Christ, heard the voice of God through a cleft in the rock and using those words wrote the Book of Revelation. You may touch the carved niches in the rock. These are said to be the places where John rested his head at night and the spot he used to help himself stand up in the morning."

Of course we touched them. The cool stone, worn smooth by countless other touches over the centuries, felt comforting. Smells of fragrant incense filled the cave and taking a moment to take it all in was worth the looks of impatience from the lines of others waiting their turn to see.

After the awe of the cave, it took several minutes for either of us to speak after leaving. Walking through the forest toward the coast, we were both deeply lost in our own thoughts.

"Do you think it's too early to find a beer?" I asked.

Cheryl looked as though I'd just given her a wedgie. "A beer? Now?"

"Sure. It's almost noon and the café's by the dock are so cute. We could stop for a quick rest and people-watch."

The beer was divine. Cold and refreshing to go along perfectly with the salty spray covering the colorful fishing boats docked close by. "Look! It's a whole family on a motor scooter," Cheryl pointed.

Sure enough – Dad driving, Mom on the back, and two children sandwiched between them. "It's the Greek equivalent of an SUV!" I snapped pictures to send back to friends at home. Sometimes people-watching is my favorite pastime!

Mykonos, Greece

Despite our early start, we couldn't slow down for long because today we were getting two Greek Islands for the price of one – Patmos in the morning and Mykonos in the afternoon.

This was one aspect of cruising life we weren't too crazy about – the appetizer-like time spent in each port. Just a tiny taste of each place. Sometimes it's fun to explore at your own pace, without having to adhere to a strict schedule. I simply had to realize organized tours with screaming children, discordant families, and bodies without benefit of a potent deodorant are to be endured if one is to partake in the blessing of bacon every morning.

Our fortuitous afternoon arrival on the island of Mykonos coincided with the arrival of another three cruise ships, all carrying substantially more cruise-clad tourists than our own boat. We joined the parade of streaming bodies like a trail of sugar ants, climbing through the tiny, white streets, not daring to step off the path for fear of being crushed by the surge.

"Keep walking," Cheryl warned. "Don't get out of the line; you'll never get back in." For a while I lost sight of her amid the walking heads. A hand reached out from behind a passing postcard stand and grabbed my arm.

"Hey," I yelled, ready to smack whoever was hiding behind the tacky tourist stuff.

"It's me," Cheryl laughed. "I had to get out of the herd for a second. I didn't see you behind me and worried you might have gotten trampled."

We waited out some of the larger crowds by perusing postcards of Greek cats and finally made a run for the nearest taverna. It was an excellent choice. The strings of octopus hung out in front, windmills on the horizon, and the brilliant sunset view across the Aegean Sea made up for the sardine-like packing we'd endured getting here.

As darkness fell and we made a more leisurely trek back to the boat, the streets were lit with blinding white lights. We saw Zorba the Greek and enormous pelicans serving as symbols of the city. We tasted Ouzo from a massive wooden barrel and enjoyed a liter of luscious Greek wine for eight euros.

Discos pumped music into the air, shops coaxed invitingly, and smiles of the beautiful Greek people soothed our earlier frayed nerves.

"It doesn't feel like we've seen enough," I complained as we boarded the ship later that evening. "This is a place we should put down on the re-vist list."

"I agree," Cheryl said. "But only for a time when the cruise ships aren't around. We need time to explore and give this island the time it deserves."

I nodded, humming a Greek tune we'd overheard in the tavern.

Izmir, Turkey

We weren't through with St. John just yet. Our trip to Izmir, Turkey would highlight both the ancient city of Ephesus and the presumed home the Virgin Mary, his charge after Jesus was crucified.

It was another of the "follow the man with the sign, line up, load the bus, give your ticket" tours. But the bus had great air conditioning, the seats were comfy, and our guide was excellent.

"If you look out the windows on either side you'll see fertile fields of cotton, tomatoes, peaches, corn, watermelons, and olives, all growing side-by-side," he explained.

"Was that your stomach?" Cheryl turned around in her seat in alarm.

"Yes it was. All this talk about food is making me hungry. Shh. He's talking." I whispered back.

Our guide continued, "High on the cliffs above stood many castle lookouts. The people could see around for miles and assumed they were always safe. The castle you see on the left was taken by force when a band of marauders tricked the settlement. It was a moonless night and those in the lookout saw hundreds of torches from troops coming up the north face of the cliff. They pulled all their forces to this area and mounted an attack.

"It was unfortunate for them while their troops were on the north side; the actual enemy crept up the south slope and destroyed the army from behind. The torches? Cleverly tied to the heads of a large herd of goats. They had no trouble climbing the cliff."

I wanted to know more about the lives of the sultans, kings, and emperors who were here and how so much history was still left undiscovered. Along the way to Ephesus we saw massive Bedouin camps alongside modern amenities like IKEA.

"Let's volunteer to help out at one of the archeological digs out here. We could learn so much," I offered.

Cheryl agreed it would be a fun thing to do, but since our time in Izmir was limited to eight hours or the boat would leave us behind in Turkey, we had to be content with a visit to the ruins of Ephesus.

"Ephesus was the capital of five hundred Anatolian towns. This was at the time when St. John lived and died. The roads of the city are paved in marble. About 250,000 people lived in this city…"

Our new guide spouted facts as quickly as he trotted through the ruins. Keeping up with his banter was almost as difficult as trying not to slip on the marble pavers as we ran past Hadrian's Temple toward the Library of Celsus.

"I think we lost another one," I shouted over my shoulder to Cheryl as another of our tour group fell by the wayside.

"She's okay," Cheryl shouted back. "She just stopped for a picture of the kitties roaming around."

Kitties? I wanted a picture of them, too. If I missed the bus and had to hoof it back to the boat on my own, so be it. At least I would bring home a picture of the cute orange kitten cavorting around the thousand year old wreckage.

While I snapped pictures, Cheryl amused herself trying to match pieces of column in an archeological jigsaw puzzle of massive proportions. All too quickly, it was time to leave Ephesus and continue on to the Virgin Mary's house.

"This isn't right," I whined. "It's like we are given just the tiniest taste of the most fantastic sweet in the world. A touch to the tongue and then it's pulled away."

"Yes, there's so much to see here and it's amazing. So much history. We'll just have to come back." That's Cheryl, always the voice of reason. For her, visiting these places was a large part of the spiritual retreat she was sought while traveling.

The site deemed by many to be the home of Jesus Christ's mother was a humble dwelling radiating a powerful energy for us as visitors. Meryem Ana Evi, or Mother Mary's House in Turkish, is nothing more than a small, restored stone cottage set in tranquil woods, overlooking the Aegean Sea. A modest home, yet it contained such significance.

Seeing the wall where hundreds of tissue and paper prayer requests were carefully tucked into the rock brought home the influence this place of pilgrimage has for both Christians and Muslims. While I was taking a few minutes to let it all sink in under an olive tree, a tiny black and white kitten tottered over to trade purrs for a rub.

"What happened to the front of your shirt? You're soaking wet," I asked as Cheryl caught up a few minutes later.

"You know the three holy fountains back there, for Health, Wealth, and Happiness? Well, I took a sip from Health and Wealth just fine, but when I got to Happiness, the water came out in a huge gush and splashed all over me! I think it was trying to tell me something."

As we rode the bus back to the boat that afternoon, she explained, "This trip. This time. This place. All these are very meaningful to me. I feel like I was meant to take this journey to find them. And a part of me that was lost."

I understood perfectly.

Santorini, Greece

Even as I write this, I'm struck by how profound my disappointment was on leaving this island. I was dejected beyond reason. Not because the visit was anything less than spectacular. The island is magical. Shades of blues and stark whites mingle in ways that make one yearn for oils and a brush. Overlooks from churches gaze into the deepest sapphire waters to bring a palette of colors the mind isn't able to forget.

I was upset because I couldn't get a picture. Not "a" picture, but "the" picture. We've all seen it. It's on all the brochures of the Greek Islands. Google Santorini and you'll see it. The Caldera overlook — a brilliant blue dome of the church against a white so whole and absolute it defines the color — all set against the backdrop of the volcanic hills and the rival cobalt of the sea.

Our tour didn't go there.

While we did walk through a quiet village and eavesdrop on a smiling woman picking flowers at her gate, saw cave houses and a weathered man peeling potatoes on his side street porch; we didn't visit the spot where I could take the picture I wanted for my screensaver forever. Even though we learned grapevines are placed close to the ground in a circle to protect the fragile fruit from the ceaseless winds and saw mountains of pistachios loaded onto the back of a small donkey; we weren't anywhere near the famous overlook.

Even the possibility of a harrowing ride down the windy mountain on a shaky cable car wasn't enough to shake me out of my funk.

"I hope we don't crash," I muttered. "This machine is centuries old. I don't want to be known as the person who brought down the famous Santorini cable car system just because I couldn't turn down a second piece of baklava at lunch."

Cheryl wisely ignored my complaining, enjoying the view of the crystal blue sea under us. As we sailed away from the Greek Islands, we watched them grow smaller behind us. "We'll be back," Cheryl said quietly. "Things feel unfinished here."

One thing we've learned on this trip is to never question those feelings.

11

"I never travel without my diary. One should always have something sensational to read in the train."

- Oscar Wilde

Rome, Italy

"Are you awake?" Cheryl asked as we sped along the Italian Autostrada. "How far are we from Rome?"

"Hmm? What? Oh yes, sorry. I'm awake now. Rome? Let me check the map."

I fumbled through the empty pistachio bags and bottled water under my feet as Cheryl continued her careful observations on the road ahead. "We just passed exit twenty-eight for the Grande Raccondo Anulare, but I'm not sure which one we should take to get us to the hostel. Do you have the directions?"

"Let me look. Here's the map. Oops, dropped it. I'll find the right page, hang on. We're looking for the E35, connecting to the Autostrada A1 north, no south. And according to this map – wait, there's a bigger map of the city in the back of the book. Let me look at it. Okay, we need the Via del Mare. Good grief, could the writing on these pages be any smaller? I don't see the Via del Mare anywhere. Have you seen any other signs?"

"I saw signs for the GRA and Autostrada back a few kilometers. We should be getting close to our exit." Cars whizzed by us at supersonic speeds. "This makes me nervous. I don't want to circle the city."

"Okay, I'll find it. Let me try another map. Wait, it's in the backseat. Never mind, I'll use this one. Well, it looks like our best bet will be to – uh-oh; the road we need doesn't go all the way through Rome. We should definitely take the GRA, it skirts the whole city. Yes, that's the one. Anything else will take us too far out of the way."

"Does it show on the map which exit it is?" Cheryl pleaded.

"Let me check. I really need a magnifying glass for this tiny writing. Okay, here it is. Exit twenty-eight is the one we need. Hey, do we have any of those pistachios left? And I will need to go to the bathroom soon. Don't close your eyes while driving!"

Hard to believe we ever made it to the hostel. Even harder to believe we actually stayed the night.

"Cheryl, why are all the buildings in Ostia covered in graffiti? It looks like a slum down here."

"Uh-huh," she said distractedly as tiny cars whizzed by on either side of us on the one lane road. "Can you see the numbers on the buildings?"

"Hard to tell. They're all covered by graffiti. Do you think this is a big gang area? I didn't read anything about gangs in the guidebook."

"There it is. Wow. Across the street from the beach, too. We've never stayed at a hostel with a beach view before."

"It looks like an abandoned building. Wait. The barbed wire gate is opening. We should park inside so our car doesn't get tagged, too."

"Tagged?"

"It's a gang term. You know, short for spray painted."

I couldn't tell whether the look I got from Cheryl was exasperation or exhaustion, but inside the hostel was a nice surprise. Once used as the Vittorio Emanuele III summer school, the enormous property is part of the Cultural Heritage Ministry of Rome. The white marble stairs were polished to a high, slippery sheen. I know this because the elevator was out and our room was on the third floor.

Echoing hallways led to an enormous dorm room. The six-person female dorm even included a tiny view of the sea from the open window. A wispy breeze barely subdued the intense heat we'd unearthed since arriving in Rome. Cool sheets beaconed and the only detail standing in the way of a welcome night's sleep was the hum of large buzzing insects looking for relief from the heat as well. If size was any indication, they also must be looking for blood. Lots of blood.

Sharing a room isn't my favorite thing about hostels, but we'd been lucky to find this dorm only occupied by one other person. She was sound asleep when we arrived.

We found out why well before dawn the next day. The pre-sunrise sounds of ripping Velcro, crinkling plastic bags, and shredding zippers mercifully brought the sweat-drenched, my-body-as-mosquito-food night to a close.

I rolled over and groaned in the direction of Cheryl's bed. "There's a mosquito bite on my butt. I have mosquito bites all over my body. They ate me alive last night."

Cheryl was nowhere to be found, but I heard the shower running. While I counted itching welts on my body – twenty-one in all – and worried if we were a malaria zone; I watched our room-mate finish packing up her belongings in a massive suitcase and struggle toward the door.

"Good morning," I said, getting up to help her with the door.

She smiled and thanked me with a warm "Merci", then thumped off for the stairs. With a suitcase as big as she was, I didn't envy her trip one bit. A French girl traveling alone to a hostel in Rome. Where was she off to next? Where had her journey taken her so far? Was she ever lonely?

Cheryl came out of the bathroom with a big smile on her face. "The shower feels great! There's no hot water, but not a problem in this heat. It's so refreshing. Are you ready to go explore Rome?"

Once again I was thankful to have someone along to share this journey with – a friend to vent at and to get frustrated with when things invariably don't go as planned; but most importantly, someone to laugh with when traveling becomes a comedy of errors and shrug it off together. The icy shower felt wonderful.

It was ridiculously easy to use public transportation from our hostel. The minutes I'd spent at breakfast agonizing (and driving Cheryl crazy) over the fact we were staying on the coast rather than Rome central were all for naught. A quick bus ride from the hostel to the train terminal costing only one Euro, taking the Metro B line directly into Rome, and there we were.

"Oh my God! Oh my God! Oh my God!" I stared in disbelief as we emerged from the bustling Colosseo train station. We were greeted by an upfront, up close – right across the street close – view of the Coliseum of Rome. Wow!

We stopped in our tracks to gawk, causing people behind us to suddenly spout Italian expletives and scuttle around. Locals, I'm sure.

The Coliseum was an enormous mountain and we were standing at base camp. "I wonder if everyone stops like that when they come out of the station?" Cheryl asked as we found a safer spot to stand and stare. I snapped pictures like a maniac. We walked around the block, soaking up each angle.

There was a sign outside proclaiming the Roman Coliseum as one of the New Seven Wonders of the World. "New Seven Wonders? What's that?" Cheryl asked a helpful English-speaking guide. We learned just a few weeks before on 7/7/2007; a consortium in Lisbon compiled over one hundred million votes to pick the Roman Coliseum, Taj Mahal, the Great Wall of China, Petra, Chichén Itzá, the Statue of Christ Redeemer, and Machu Picchu as the New Seven Wonders of the World.

"This should be a topic of one of our books," Cheryl shouted over the roar of cars shooting through the Via Dei Fori Imperiali. "We should write a *What Boundaries?* book about these New Seven Wonders."

"Guess it means we'll have to visit them all," I yelled back as we took our lives into our hands and crossed the Via Claudia to catch one of the waiting Hop-On, Hop-Off Tour buses. Panting from the sheer terror of traversing a busy street in Rome and sweating profusely from the powerful heat radiating from under our feet, we jumped on the first bus as it pulled from the curb.

"Where does this one go?" I asked while trying to breathe huge gulps of super-heated air and not pass out at the same time.

"Not sure, but at least we're moving." Cheryl gasped back as the Arch of Constantine loomed to our right. We did the usual tour. Pull out the map. Get a good overview of the city while on the bus, then mark the places we wanted to see more of. Soon my map was full of marks. Piazza Navona, the Vatican with all nine miles of museums, Spanish Steps, Trevi Fountain, Pantheon, the Forum, Circus Maximus, as well as all the churches and fountains mentioned in Angels and Demons.

"Why are we stopping? We've only covered half the map." I asked as our driver exited at Termini station where everyone around us leisurely collected their belongings and trundled off into the crowds. Our bus was lined up behind two others and being reluctant to give up top deck seats where the headphones actually worked, we decided to wait.

After ten minutes in the baking heat, the first bus left and we inched forward to fill the space. Other passengers came aboard and within a few minutes all the seats were full. The throngs of tourists visiting Rome in August amazed me. It is wall-to-wall people and so hot you could barely think. Why would anyone visit Rome in August? Why were we here in August? What's wrong with us?

I'm not sure why we had so much affection for this particular bus, but perhaps it was lethargy from the heat keeping us dripping in our seats for nearly an hour. I'm sure Termini Station is an interesting place as seen from the top of a double-decker bus, but on this day, I was too hot to notice. When we finally pulled away from the curb, my skin drank up the breeze like a gasping fish.

Soon we crossed the Tiber, immersed in the spectacle of Rome, lost in thoughts of the most powerful kingdom of all time. Rulers who made decisions affecting time forward and yet in many places here it seems as though time has stopped in its tracks. We learned the reason there were only two metro lines was because important ancient ruins keep being discovered when new lines are attempted.

In the middle of a busy street, traffic is rerouted around a new archeological dig. "I'd like to be a part of an archeological dig someday," I mused out loud. After our visit to Ephesus, I was imagining a second career as an archeologist.

"That would be fun. Is it okay if we find some place cooler than Rome?" Cheryl asked as the bus suddenly lurched, making a sickening scraping sound as metal met concrete. "Whoa, what did we hit?"

As we had just turned onto Via Della Conciliazione and were within site of the Vatican, most people on the tour were busy snapping pictures of the basilica dome, oblivious to the damaged bus now sitting atop the curb.

With our seats tilted at an odd angle, we watched as the Italian driver below jumped out, started waving his arms and shouting insanely – at the bus. He cursed and kicked and if anything moveable had been within reach I'm sure he would have thrown it for good measure.

A group of nuns watched the show from the sidewalk, giving thanks I'm sure for the fact the errant bus hadn't jumped the curb just moments before as they'd strolled by.

It appeared no one was hurt, though the crumpled fender of the bus left it unable to be driven. So in short order a new one was summoned. Twenty more minutes waiting in the heat, but the view of St. Peter's Basilica was breathtaking and we got some amazing pictures.

By this time I quite over sightseeing and all it took was for Cheryl to say the words "potato skins" and I grinning like an idiot. She'd already spotted it on the map – Hard Rock Café Rome!

Walking in from the hot street was like steeping into a refrigerated oasis… and then we had the potato skins. And Buffalo wings, Buffalo strips, nachos, and onion rings! We pigged out in total American junk food heaven. The Hard Rock was totally against our credo of eating authentic foods in each country we visited, but we blamed it all on the heat.

For two more days we explored the streets of Rome; tossing coins into Trevi Fountain, climbing steps to views commanding the city, eating pizza in cafes having nothing to do with rock and roll, writing copious notes and taking so many pictures of marble it seemed as though my eyes would break. By the third day we were wilted and unrecognizable.

"I can't cope with this heat anymore," I moaned. We'd been spending eight to ten hours a day outside sightseeing and it finally caught up with us.

"We're staying across the street from the beach. Why don't we call tomorrow a 'beach day', hang out at the hostel and take in some down time while it's windy at the shore." Cheryl's suggestion was music to my ears.

Being cool sounded like heaven to me and it turned out to be a great opportunity to meet others staying at the hostel. Paulien from the Netherlands and Anja visiting from Germany were curious what we were up to working so intensely on our computer. When we told them we were writing a book about our travels, they wanted to know more. An afternoon of great conversation turned into a multicultural dinner on the beach. They too had decided to take a day off from sightseeing and enjoy the cool breezes from the ocean. Talking with people from different counties and batting around ideas is a gift hostels provide for those willing to let themselves open up. I'm not usually good at doing this, but thankfully Cheryl is.

We spent lots of time trying to explain our American government and how it works – as they were fascinated by our leaders and knew so much more about ours than we did of theirs. Both spoke excellent English (it is required in their schools) and Anja spoke three other languages fluently as well.

Customs were another topic of conversation. Anja had us all laughing as she described the way she and her friends greeted each other.

"Do you hug?" asked Paulien.

"Oh no!" she said in horror. "We extend our arm and shake hands. Like this." It was hilarious to watch her demonstrate this stiff-armed, mechanical expression of greeting.

Decadent gelatos, a cold bottle of Pinot Grigio, and a free jazz concert on the Ostia beach rounded out our stay in Rome. Notes from haunting saxophone music on the waves were the background as we made plans to meet up again with Paulien in Florence the next week – as though we'd known each other for years.

Saying goodbye to Anja the next morning, I reached out my hand for her to shake, but she came right up and gave me a big hug, smiling the whole time. American, German, and Dutch in Italy – the lines between us seem much blurrier here!

12

"Traveling is the ruin of all happiness! There's no looking at a building after seeing Italy."

- Fanny Burney

Florence, Italy

Florence is a feast for the senses. But by the time we arrived, our senses were somewhere between beaten, bedraggled and spent. The city welcomed us anyway.

"How could we have gotten so lost?" Cheryl propped her elbows on the table in utter exhaustion, cradling a glass of vino rosso. "We drove around for hours trying to find the hostel and it turns out we were passing it again and again."

"It's the street signs," I said, nibbling a corner of bruschetta so vibrant in color it could be the centerfold of a food magazine. "There's one name on the street for a while and something different a few blocks later. We were looking for Via Nazionale, but we were on Largo Fratelli Alinari. How could we know it was the same road?" Our prayers to St. Anthony, patron saint of lost souls, had obviously gone unheeded. This was our only excuse.

The drive from Rome had been a glorious jaunt through the heart of Tuscany. Rolling hills, vineyards stretching for miles, sunflowers in repose – it was everything I'd dreamt of and more.

Arriving in Florence just after one in the afternoon, we expected to be firmly ensconced in our hostel by two, at the latest. By four we were barely able to speak to each other for fear of crushing already frayed nerves.

"I don't know where we are," I snapped. "The road we're driving on isn't on this map. Not one of these roads is."

Cheryl was trying her best to dodge traffic, buzzing motorbikes, and darting pedestrians while I tried to read the street signs flashing by on both sides. We just wanted to be out of the car.

"Wait! The road we just passed. I see it here on the map. We're not too far away now. A few minutes at the most."

Half hour later, I saw another familiar street on the map. "It's Via Flume. The hostel should be right over there." I pointed as we whizzed by a monstrous building.

"I'll circle the block," Cheryl offered. "Can you jump out and check to see if it's the right place? I don't see any signs on the outside."

Circling the block in busy Florence isn't the easiest feat, especially when the traffic lava flow all seems to want to be somewhere else. Well, so did we.

"I can't wait for that first glass of wine."

"Glass? Just bring me the bottle."

Cheryl double-parked for a second while I tried to find a sliver of space between oncoming traffic to dart through. Jumping out of the car, I almost hit the pavement hard. After sitting in the car for so long, my butt was completely numb. I could see Cheryl chuckling at my loping gait from the window.

The building resembled a foreboding castle – grimy and dark-faced from the exhaust of thousands of cars. There was a buzzer and small sign suggesting this was indeed the hostel. A male voice answered in Italian. I asked about our reservation, the one made online several weeks before.

The scratchy voice from the building spoke again, this time in English. "Come up. Third floor. Take the lift." Then the gargantuan front door swung open. I peered inside at the gloomy entrance, noting a few dusty bikes and a tiny, rickety elevator constructed sometime in the mid-1400s.

I made sure Cheryl saw me go inside; waving feebly in case this was a last memory as I disappeared into the building. A gust of wind caught the big doors and I had seconds to jump out of the way, trying not to get crushed when they slammed hard behind me.

Now it nearly pitch dark and I was on my own to figure out how to use this fragile piece of metal to lift me up to the third floor. Stepping inside, I pushed the requisite button and after some agonizing moments of clanking and groaning (from the elevator, not me this time), absolutely nothing happened.

I pushed more buttons. Still nothing. Shadows from the silent stairwell grew larger and dusty trails of sweat started running down my neck.

I was still standing in the lift mulling over taking the scary stairs instead when the massive doors blew open once again and Cheryl appeared, backlit like an angel.

"Hey," she said. "I parked around the corner. Have you talked to anyone yet?"

"I can't get this lift to work." I said miserably.

"Oh. Let me look." She climbed in, looked around the cage for a minute, pulled an invisible door from the wall and up we went. "Did you push all the buttons on purpose?" she asked as we took a floor-by-floor tour.

We laughed about it now as the waiter brought our dinner – tagliatelle bolognaise with porcini mushrooms for me, while Cheryl dug into the rich tortellini carbonara. The side order of garlic sautéed spinach soon followed. It was divine.

"You looked so pitiful standing there in the lift. In the dark." The road weariness was dissolving in direct proportion to the amount of Chianti we consumed.

"Yes, thank you for not mentioning how stupid I was for not realizing the door had to be closed before the elevator would work."

"Here in Italy they're called lifts and aren't anything like any elevator we've ever used before."

An hour later, tummies full beyond measure, we were ready to leave the comfort of the restaurant and face the streets of Florence again. This time for pistachio gelato.

"Tooth check," I said, baring my teeth in lion-like fashion.

"Clear. No spinach in your teeth. You're good to talk to people without embarrassment. How are mine?"

Having a good friend along to share the adventures of travel is priceless. To get me out of sticky lift situations – and especially when she finds a late night grocery selling bottles of Ruffino Chianti for four euros each!

Waking up in a new city to the sound of bells outside the window is normally a balm for travel-frayed tensions – until you realize it's only five AM.

"Wow, those are loud," Cheryl said, pulling back heavy wooden shutters. We were struck dumb by the sheer beauty of this small corner of Florence we could see from our window. Dawn streaked the sky and the light was delicate on the stones. The bells belonged to the Basilica di Santa Maria Novella, calling the faithful to Mass. Even at this hour of the morning, the circle pulsed with life. Cars whizzed by, bikes dodged shoppers piled high with bags, and tourists trundled heavy bags in the direction of the train station. In the background, just barely visible was the magnificent Duomo. Even from this distance, it was breathtaking.

A day of exploration awaited – senses were now on full absorb mode. Firenze (Florence) met us with a full military parade by our door. Goose-bump producing bands and pageantry marched by as we applauded enthusiastically, even if we couldn't understand all the words being spoken around us.

What would a visit to a new city be without the requisite Hop On, Hop Off bus tour? Seeing the busy streets in relative safety from high atop a double-decker bus gave a new appreciation of the craziness of driving here in Florence.

The coolness of Santa Croce beckoned us as the afternoon sun became too much to bear. Here tombs of Galileo, Michelangelo, and Machiavelli dwell in eternal rest beside the Medici Chapel. These were breathtaking examples of expression – pain and rapture – so moving it could soften the hardest heart.

We learned Michelangelo, in his genius, believed the stone spoke to him, revealing what it should be sculpted. As such, he claimed to be only the stonecutter who brought out hidden form, not an artist at all.

Firenze is noted as the "most Tuscan city" in Tuscany. With sidewalk cafés and pizzerias, knock-off Prada bags, miles of Murano glass, and so much leather I felt sad for Elsie – we were kept busy for hours shopping for presents to send back home.

We munched on a late lunch at Loggio. Quattro Seasonale – stone-fired pizza with the edges so crispy it tasted like the outside of a campfire marshmallow left too long in the flames. And vino rosso, of course. As satisfied as pampered housecats, we walked back along the River Arno through Ponte Vecchio and deep into the streets of Firenze.

We ducked into a bookstore, cool and redolent with the smell of old literature. I closed my eyes in a moment of pure ecstasy, until I realized I'd been mistaken. I wasn't in Heaven, but rather in Dante's Third Level of Hell. There were books by the thousands. I could look at the books. Touch the books. Even smell the books, but I couldn't read any of them. They were all in Italian.

This had happened before in a few smaller European bookstores, dusty cellars, and in the riverside carts along the Seine. I'd wander aimlessly, touching and flipping through covers, but never with this many books to choose from. As tears were starting to well up, Cheryl appeared with a huge grin on her face.

"Upstairs," she whispered. "Upstairs they have section of books in English!"

Not about to take another chance with a lift, I doubt I've ever climbed stairs so fast before. The books we'd brought with us originally had long been sucked dry. Anything in English we could trade for at a hostel was welcome. But our book pantry had long since run dry and I was a book addict in search of a fix.

"Wow, Cheryl," I cried in alarm, "books are so expensive in Italy!"

"So it's not in the budget. Don't worry about it. Get the books you want." Walking out of the store with two Leonardo Da Vinci biographies and a mindless mystery to pass the time when our fingers cramped from writing in journals was a highlight of my time in Florence.

On a whim, we took an early morning bus to the town of Fiosole. High on a hill overlooking the city of Florence and its adjacent groves, we sat enjoying morning espresso and a plate of simple caprese salad. Warm tomatoes, thick slices of buttery mozzarella, and olive oil so thick with the taste of Tuscany I almost fainted.

"Stop licking the basil leaves. Leave some olive oil for me," Cheryl laughingly scolded.

With great reluctance, I pushed the plate back in her direction, my eyes still glazed from the ability of the Italians to pack so much culinary excellence into such basic things. Whether it's an olive oil from the fattoria (I love saying that word!), infused with herbs capturing the boldness of rosemary and a hint of anise to lasagna with paper thin layers of pasta and a sauce so sweet my eyes roll back into my head.

Our last night in Florence, we arranged to meet up with our friend Paulien from Rome. She was on her final stop before heading home to the Netherlands. She'd come from Sienna the night before and soon had us laughing again at how a seemingly simple trip can have so many twists and turns.

We walked from Piazzo Duomo to Loggio (again) for pizza, pasta and wine. After dinner, we stumbled on a large crowd beside the Uffizi Gallery (not unusual in the daylight, but now it was after ten PM). It wasn't Michelangelo's statue of David that drew us in, but haunting sound of a flute on the night air.

It was an impromptu street concert with the flutist giving way to a couple beautifully singing renditions of Simon and Garfunkel favorites. The lighted statues of Leonardo, Dante, Medici, along with their ensemble of greats stood high above the Piazza della Signoria in watchful waiting.

The crowd must have numbered in the hundreds; walkers out to taste the city at night, those strolling by with a gelato or a cigarette, families with children playing in the square. The air was perfectly cool and it seemed as though the stars were listening, too. We stood there together for nearly an hour and enjoyed the music so much we bought a CD to remember our last beautiful night in Firenze.

Greve in Chianti

The drive through this area of Italy was so beautiful I almost didn't want to find our destination. Almost.

At one point the view was just too much to let pass us by. We pulled over to take pictures of the glowing Sangiovese grapes growing en masse along the road. Olive trees grew so close you could smell their warm, dusky leaves. Row upon row of knarled and knotted olive trunks stood alongside grapevines, their lines stretching for miles across rolling hills dotted with stone farmhouses painted burnt yellow or blazing with an orange tile roof. Colors smolder and seethe here. A blast of white assaults the eyes from laundry hung out windows to dry.

Greve is an adorable village. Our first stop led us downstairs to a veritable Christmas morning for wine lovers. In Le Cantine di Greve in Chianti, it's possible to do a tasting of wine, cheese, grappa, and olive oil. Over one hundred forty varieties of wine are there for tasting! We were in heaven. A wine-card is purchased for ten or twenty euros and each taste costs forty cents to four euros, depending on the price of the bottle. Bread and olive oils from their own fattoria were also available. I think I enjoyed the olive oils nearly as much as the wine. Well, it was a close second.

Dragging me out of there was tough, but Cheryl promised a visit to the Corkscrew Museum on the way out. How often do you get to see one of those?

Lunch was at a restaurant whose specialty was pasta with wild pig sauce. Holey Moley, I could have eaten three plates of it! The sauce was divinely inspired – peppercorns, spices and a sauce so savory it took all I had not to pick up the plate and lick it clean. For Cheryl's sake (and what little dignity I still kept), I held back.

As we walked back to our car, we stopped in for water at a small shop. The sweet Italian lady busy stocking the shelves explained she had just bought the store and it wasn't due to open until ten AM the next day, but if we saw anything we wanted she'd be happy to ring it for us. Of course, we had to add our best wishes to the three bottles of Greve Chianti we happily took with us to Vinci.

Vinci, Italy

We came to this town, like so many others before us, in search Leonardo Da Vinci's spirit. For a taste of the air he breathed and the vistas that inspired and shaped his young life.

There weren't any hostels or hotels available on-line in Vinci, so we went for the next closest town of Spogliano, opting to drive the few kilometers into Vinci for ghost hunting.

Jackpot on the hotel – yes, a real HOTEL – with our own private shower and beds with no noticeable sag in the middle. Bonus features of wood floors, track lighting and a flat screened television had us feeling as though we'd stepped through the Looking Glass.

Everything about the town of Vinci was delightful in a kind and simplistic way. First stop was Leonardo's childhood home in Anchiano and presumably the place where he was born. Parking down the lane among the olive groves, it's a short walk up a flagstone path with cicadas loudly announcing our arrival.

Such a small home, but the view is breathtaking. Rolling hills, soaring forests with trees so high I was dizzy looking up – no wonder this man wanted to fly. I wanted to fly and I was just standing there admiring the view.

We shared our time at the house with a lady using polio braces to walk carefully through the gardens. I sipped icy water from both the cistern at the top and bottom of the hill – just in case something is in the water here.

We walked through the olive groves, getting lost in the silvery mist of leaves. Was there some whisper of this man still left in those shadows? I was moved by the simplicity and mystery of the place.

Visits to the museum, Leonardo's Library, and the Santa Croce Parish Church where he was baptized rounded out a day of da Vinci.

On the way back to our hotel in Spogliano we stopped for some basics at the grocery. Limoncello, water, and soda were on the list. Also, it had been seven weeks on the road and the gray was threatening to take over my hair. So I picked up a bottle hair color.

"Is that the same brand you use back home?" Cheryl asked.

"No. But it looks about the same shade as mine. What do you think?"

Being blessed with blonde locks that never required a touch-up to keep their original color, Cheryl didn't understand why I was so adamant about keeping the grays at bay. "I guess it's the right color, but the instructions are in Italian. Are you sure you'll know how to do it?"

"All hair color is the same. Leave it on for a half hour and rinse it out. I've got a few more grays than usual, so I'll leave it on a few minutes extra. I'm sure it'll be fine." I replied confidently.

My confidence turned to horror as I stared into the hotel mirror later that night. Even an extra shot of limoncello couldn't blunt the shock. From every angle it simply got worse.

Laughing uproariously from the bed, Cheryl put in her own two cents. "I think you've nailed it perfectly. Your hair is the exact shade of merlot on fire – bright purple with just a subtle hint of red. Women all over Europe will be killing to copy that shade. Just watch."

Purple hair. My newest traveling companion. I buried my head in a pillow and tried to calculate how many times I could safely wash my hair in a day before it all fell out. At least that might be an improvement.

13

"Tourists don't know where they've been, travelers don't know where they're going."

- Paul Theroux

Venice, Italy

"You're kidding, right?" I asked as I read over the directions to our next destination. "We're really staying at a place called the Jolly Campground?"

"You had a good time the last time we stayed at a campground. It's a great price and here we'll stay in a travel trailer with air conditioning. No tent, I promise."

"But it's called Jolly," I muttered. A travel trailer was definitely better than a tent and air con sounded wonderful right now. It was sweltering in Venice in August. As we drove into the Jolly, the sight of a charming pizzeria and massive swimming pool quelled all my fears about another camping adventure. This would be a nice change.

We checked in and were given our key and directions to the trailer. "Look at this, if you wear your underwear to the bar between ten and midnight, you get twenty percent off of your drinks," I read from the Camping Jolly brochure.

"If you want to get a drink in your underwear, go right ahead. And do you think you'll be awake at ten?" She was right. It had been a long ride across Italy from Florence. The mountains were spectacular to view, but slow going to drive through. If it weren't for the absolute need for doing laundry and trying out the local pizza, I'd have crawled into the bed and savored the ice cold air conditioning.

However, as we unpacked our things and realized the clothes on our backs were the last clean things we owned, laundry became our first priority.

"Hey, look. The machines are outside." I was amazed. I hadn't seen washers and dryer outside before. I was obviously a camping newbie. Cheryl offered to start the first load if I'd go get us a seat at the rapidly filling pizzeria and order a bottle of wine. I was very okay with this arrangement.

The chilled bottle of vino bianchi arrived. The cold, crisp taste was just what we needed to revive. At this rate, we might even be able to make the ten o'clock underwear happy hour. Mouth-watering aromas of pizza and the scent of sunscreen from pool splashers wafted over candlelit tables. A young couple came in and after looking around for an empty table, started to leave. We were seated at a large table, so offered to share it with them.

He was biking alone on an adventure through Italy, the Czech Republic, and Poland. We talked bikes for a while, as I missed being on mine back home. He'd bought his especially to hold the seventy pounds of gear he needed for this journey. And I thought my pack was heavy.

"So what made you decide to take this kind of trip?" It was nice to ask someone else the same question we'd been asked repeatedly since leaving home.

"One of my professors from Uni – I'm in my gap year now – said she'd taken the same route and it changed her life. I wanted the same experience."

"Has it been difficult for you? Riding all alone?"

"Not so much. Before I started, I'd only ridden my bike to school, about a mile or so. Now I'm doing seventy to a hundred miles a day. My biggest turning point came when I was struggling every day for two weeks, then it became easy. I realized I was getting into shape!"

Our pizza arrived along with theirs, a salad and two sides of spaghetti. "Wow, you guys must be hungry." I couldn't help but stare at the mountain of food.

He laughed. "The salad is hers. The pizza we'll share. The pasta is all for me. When I'm riding, I burn about three to four thousand calories a day just to sustain the pace I've set. My typical foods are Snickers bars and pasta whenever I can find it. I ride all day, following the riverbeds, and pitch a tent at night. I'll find a WC in a petrol station and wash my clothes. I tie them to the back of the bike to dry as I ride, so you can imagine some of the looks I get from people as they pass me on the roadway."

"How do you find your way?" I asked.

"I find an Internet café and print out maps from Google a week in advance. This way I'm sure I've got the latest road condition information. I don't want to find a road closed and have to backtrack through the mountains."

Cheryl and I were fascinated by his story. A true road warrior, though his girlfriend seemed more bored than interested in his journey. We peppered him with a few more questions while she studied the brochures for Florence and Venice. Trying to include her in the conversation was like pulling nails, though we did find she had flown in the day before and was ready to explore Italy by car and wanted nothing at all to do with a bicycle. We wished them both luck with their adventure and went to check in on the two loads of laundry we'd been tending.

The campground fees may have been inexpensive, but doing laundry on-site certainly was not. At three euros fifty cents for each wash and dry, we were disappointed to find the dryer held still very soggy clothes, even after two cycles.

"This isn't even all our clothes. Everything was dirty." Cheryl explained.

"What are we going to do with these," I asked mid-yawn. "They are soaking wet."

"I don't think we should waste more money. Let's take them back to the room and hang them up. They'll dry by morning."

Thus began our own episode of the Beverly Hillbillies – underwear strung up beside tie-dyed t-shirts, covering every square inch of space in the tiny travel trailer.

"It's a good thing we brought the clothes line," I said sarcastically as I ducked under wet bras dangling from closet doors. "How do I get to the bathroom with all these clothes hanging everywhere?"

"Be careful not to run into the…oops. I hung clothes in the WC, too." Cheryl laughed as I stumbled into a face full of wet shorts. She could afford to be cheery; she'd made it to her bed without any zipper marks on the face.

By the time I found my way to my own bed, I had to laugh, too. "What have we become? Would you have ever thought we'd be in a trailer in a campground? Surrounded by wet clothes that wouldn't dry in the outside dryer? What happened to us?"

"Would you have ever believed we'd be having this much fun? In Venice, Italy, of all places?" Cheryl asked.

She was right, of course. Our lives now were filled with much less worry and so much laughter it was hard to imagine we were the same people who'd started out just a few weeks before. Though sometimes we take living in a relaxed manner to an extreme, traveling is suiting us well.

I could tell Cheryl was relaxing a little, because after Venice she hadn't worried about booking a place for us to stay. This included our route across Italy and France until we would arrive in Bayonne. "You realize we're going totally by the seat of our pants for the next seven days?" I asked over the hum of the air conditioner.

"Don't remind me. I won't be able to sleep. I'll have to go log onto a computer somewhere."

"I'm proud of you for being so spontaneous. When we leave here, it will be the first time in seven weeks we haven't been pre-booked somewhere."

"Enough. Now I'm worried we'll have to sleep in the car or something. Somewhere in a field in the middle of France…"

"Would that be so bad?" I asked, but she was already asleep.

Visiting the city of Venice was bit of a challenge. Being a campground and all, Jolly wasn't actually anywhere near the Venice we were expecting. Asking for directions was problematic as we spoke limited Italian and the lady at guest registry did not appear to be fond of tourists – if the huge line of campers waiting on her services was any indication.

"Could you repeat what you just said?" I asked while frantically trying to write down her rapid mixture of Italian and English words on a napkin I somehow still had in my pocket from breakfast. In three seconds, my time was up and I was dismissed with a wave.

"I've got it. I think she said we should go to the train station and take the train to the pizzeria restaurant. She said something about a pizza margarita. Maybe it's her favorite? Restaurant fare costs two euros. Then in twenty minutes we'll be in Venice." I read back from the napkin.

"Huh?" Cheryl asked with a bewildered look I now associated solely with me and directions.

A helpful, dreadlocked camper, waiting his turn behind us, stepped in, "What she actually said was, 'You'll find the bus stop just past the train station. The stop is in front of the pizza restaurant. The bus stop is called Marghera and it costs two euros each for bus fare. The bus comes every twenty minutes to take you into Venice.'" He smiled, dimples showing, "This will get you into Venice, but you're on your own for the pizza."

On the twenty minute bus ride into Venice, we prepared for the sightseeing adventure to come.

"Did you know Venice has 118 islands and over 150 canals?" Cheryl asked over the top of her guidebook.

"No fair. You've got the only Venice guide we brought. All I have is an Italian newspaper left on the seat."

"Oh, and you'll like this. By 1482, Venice was the printing capital of the world. The first paperback book was invented here. A man named Aldus Manutius produced portable books, so they could be carried in a saddlebag."

"I'll bet they would have gone crazy for the Amazon Kindle, fifteen hundred books on one little machine." I sighed wistfully. I'd been eyeing the Kindle online for the past few weeks, but couldn't yet justify the hefty price tag.

"There are over four hundred bridges in Venice," Cheryl continued, trying to ignore me. She'd been hearing me extol the virtues of an electronic book device over the heavy tomes we'd been toting around for the past few weeks. I'm sure I was starting to sound like a broken record. "The most famous bridge is the Ponte dei Sospiri or the Bridge of Sighs," she pointed out.

"Why is it called that?"

"I'm happy you asked," she said. Though I'm sure she was happier I got off the subject of an e-book reader before launching into my "perils and pitfalls of printing paper books" speech. "Lord Byron gave the bridge its name because this would be the last view of the beautiful city of Venice prisoners would see before being put into jail. The bridge connects the old prison to the interrogation rooms of the Doge's Palace."

"Ah, what a romantic name. The Bridge of Sighs." I imagined sorrowful expressions of remorse and Italian ladies crying in the background.

"Yes, unless you were a prisoner," she said. Very true.

We'd picked a good day to explore Venice. The acqua alta or "high water" proving quite a nuisance the previous week had crept back to normal levels. Though it was still a surprise to see normal entrances of homes, businesses, and even churches just inches above the lapping water.

The police, ambulance, taxi, and even pizza delivery boats were whizzing by on the canals. Stepping onto a place where all form of transport is on foot or by water is a bit disconcerting at first. This was the first major city where the Hop-On, Hop-Off Bus wasn't an option. The motorized waterbuses (vaporetti) offered to quickly whisk us where we needed to go, but it was much more fun to walk – even though we felt like the sidewalks were baking us alive.

"Let's stop for a gelato," I offered after we'd been walking all of five minutes. "It'll cool us off." Italian gelato is so incredibly delicious it should be illegal – though I'd have taken a night across the Bridge of Sighs for a third scoop of pistachio.

Watching theatrical gondoliers enunciate Italian operettas while managing to dodge swerving vaporetti loaded with camcorder-wielding Japanese tourists was worth a few minutes roasting in the sun. A gondola ride on the Grand Canal was on my "must-do" list – until we found out the cost was one hundred euros for a twenty-five minute ride.

"Yikes, that's expensive," I yelped. Our rapidly-dwindling backpacker budget would be taking a big hit.

Cheryl, as usual, came up with an ideal solution. "Why don't we take some of that money and splurge on a fantastic dinner on the canal. We can watch the boats go by and you can order the steak you've been drooling over."

We found a perfect spot on a side canal, so close to the water I felt it splash on my sandal-clad toes. A caprese salad and liter of house bianchi came as we sat back to watch the show. A grizzled old-timer and his two dogs putted by on a tiny skiff, heading out for an errand or just an evening jaunt. A family of three sped by on a sleek teak racer.

"Wonder where they're off to in such a hurry?" I asked between bites of beef filet with creamy peppercorn sauce. Before the grilled vegetables arrived, I had my answer. Coming from the opposite direction, with a distinctive flat box propped on the bow, the family boat rushed by again.

"Pizza delivery! Venice style!" We both cracked up and our waiter cautiously approached to be sure everything was all right. It was a grand evening in Venice and everything was very much all right.

Before we left The Jolly on our trek across Italy, we decided to do one more load of laundry. It must be something about the hope of travelers, but we faithfully put in our coins and somehow were still disappointed when the dryer failed to dry our underclothes to a condition any better than they were coming out of the washer.

"They're still wet," I said, trying to shake off a faint sense of déjà vu. This time we carried the soggy wad back to the trailer without a word. Our faith in the ability of dryers to do their job was shaken to the core. "Do you think these will dry by tomorrow?" I asked, wringing with all my might.

"I'm sure they will," Cheryl said confidently.

As we'd quickly learned while traveling together, confidence isn't a mistress to be teased. An early morning drive awaited us if we were to get across the mountains toward Turin, our planned next stop. The welcome coolness from the air conditioner had kept us happy all night, but didn't do much for our wet underclothes.

"The bras are still soaked. And ice cold. I'm not wearing one today, it would be like standing in a freezer."

Cheryl looked at me as though I had two heads. Not wearing a bra was something she'd never consider, but my lack of cleavage provided an unnoticeable option.

"We'll have to rig something up in the car to dry out everything," she said, already digging through our assorted stuff for a MacGuiver-like solution to the problem. Within a few minutes, she had the clothes line stretched across the back seat from window to window, secured with duct tape for the long journey ahead.

"Oh my God! What is this thing? Now we really do look like the Beverly Hillbillies!" I stared in horror at all our unmentionables dangling in the breeze.

"I know. I can't believe we have to do this. You know I'd just as soon leave a suitcase in the airport if it would ever come off the carousel open and my underwear was spilling out."

Cheryl's confession now had me imagining the worst. "What if we get caught speeding? Can you picture being pulled over on the Autostrada and having to explain why our underwear is blowing in the wind?"

"The answer my friend is blowing in the wind…no, sorry officer, it's our underwear blowing in the wind." So her Peter, Paul and Mary rendition was a little off, but it was okay. If we couldn't laugh about this now, we knew we'd be able to later.

Susa, Italy

"The dog's name is Novella, it means cloud. When she was a puppy, she was nothing but a white ball of fluff," our host informed us. But by the time she finally pulled her muddy head out of the culvert where she'd holed up a rabbit; the friendly Shepard mix more closely resembled snow on the Garden State Parkway exit ramps.

The muck and stinkyness didn't matter a bit to us as it had been quite a while since we'd had a proper "doggie fix". Novella was more than willing to aid our therapy by rolling on her back and allowing unlimited rubs and pets.

"She comes with the room," it was explained as we checked into one of the most charming places we'd stayed so far – the El Dorado Bed and Breakfast in Susa, Italy. Our plan had been to find a place to stay in Turin and start for France early the next day. Sometimes better things are in wait.

At the tourist information booth in Turin, we asked about places to stay. Late summer vacationers were in force and the number of healthy hikers and climbers in one place was staggering. All the reasonably-priced inns in this charming town were taken and paying 300 euros to stay just one night wasn't an option. "But if you're willing to drive just a little farther, there is a nice place with a room in Susa," the busy clerk explained. "It's a bed and breakfast and I'll be happy to call ahead for you."

The price was right and this being our first time venturing out of the safe confines of pre-booked travel; we agreed to take a chance. A call was made, directions given, and within a few minutes we were off to find the El Dorado.

Twenty minutes later, we realized why this place wasn't on any tourist map or online reservation service; it was barely on the map.

"We can drive by and if it looks too awful, we'll keep going. I'm sure something else will turn up," Cheryl offered.

Miles and miles of jaw-dropping mountain peaks surrounded us as we ventured down tiny farm roads; sure we'd been given the wrong information. "This is gorgeous, but we're in the middle of a farm," I couldn't help but notice as we were almost sideswiped by a hay-baler making a sudden appearance from a passing field. "Wait! Turn here. This must be it."

Sitting high on the side of a hill was a spacious chalet with a sign out front proclaiming Eldorado Bar Albergo Ristorante. "This is the place!" I shouted excitedly. "That's it. The Eldorado. We found it."

"Lisa, it's a bar and restaurant. Not a bed and breakfast. Maybe the clerk misunderstood what we were looking for."

"This has to be the right place. There can't be two El Dorado's way out here in the middle of nowhere." I tried to be hopeful, but the quantity of trucks parked in the lot, the music from a hidden patio, and several dirt-caked farmers clutching long-neck beers had me doubting my initial excitement.

"I'll go check," Cheryl proposed. It was either that or sit in the car and watch the now staring bar patrons drink beer by their trucks. I ventured a wave and was rewarded by toothy smiles from the group. My opinion of Italian farmers went up exponentially. My opinion of the El Dorado went up, too, as Cheryl came back to the car with a wide grin on her face. "This is it. They've just started to rent rooms in the big house. The bar is outside and they promised the music wouldn't be playing late. They have a wine cellar and tiny restaurant inside. And once we're settled in our room, they're providing a special welcome gift for us on the patio."

The room was immaculate with a balcony overlooking a mountain vista almost too pretty for words. From the window, the sound of rushing water was like a salve to our car-weary bodies. "Let's go explore," we said at the same time. A short hike across the street and we were in a meadow where the smell of just-plucked tomato plants was intoxicating. Deeper into the forest we went, pulled by the sound of the thundering water. Shadows were getting longer and the vegetation thicker, so we had to turn back before finding the source. As we crossed the meadow again, a family of white-tailed foxes came out for a twilight greeting.

When we joined the innkeeper and his wife out on the patio, they brought out a welcome plate of freshly baked crusty bread and mountains of thin-sliced salami – perfect to go with a bottle of wine we'd ordered from the bar.

"Since we're being spontaneous, why don't we stay here for a few more nights?" Cheryl posed. "We'll still be on track for getting to Spain for La Tomatina in two weeks, but there seems to be so much to explore here. And it's so beautiful."

I readily agreed even before she went up to the room to bring back a second bottle of wine from our Chianti stock.

Standing on our patio later in the evening, I watched the sky come alive. At first just absolute darkness, but within a few blinks the entire sky was filled with a festival of twinkling pinpricks. "Cheryl, come look at this," I was marveling at a white cross on the side of a neighboring mountain. The stark illumination of a cross surrounded by the intense blackness of the mountain created a surreal scene. Who would see this incredible light?

She appeared a few minutes later and when I pointed in the direction of the cross, it wasn't there. "Are you sure you didn't have too much wine? There's nothing out there except dark." Now she believed I was hallucinating.

"No, there was a white cross up on the mountain." I pointed at the inky blackness. "It was there."

"Uh-huh, sure it was," she agreed skeptically.

Thankfully, she had the patience to hang out a little while longer. Twenty minutes later, the light reappeared. On a timer, perhaps? "See, I told you it was there," I said smugly, shivering from the chill, but now a bit surer of my sanity. It was a colder night than we'd experienced in a long time and such a welcome change.

It was true Novella came with the room – she slept just outside our door. The first morning was a bit unnerving as my dream of an enormous mountain Yeti stalking us with dripping fangs was still lingering in the predawn light. "Cheryl! Wake up. What's outside the door? There's something big and furry blocking our door."

"Hmm?" She mumbled, pulling up her cocoon of blankets against the chilly mountain air. "What? There's no one at the door. Go back to sleep."

I could clearly see a lump in front of the door. I watched it from the safety of my bed for a few minutes, trying to convince myself this creature was way too small for a Yeti. Finally summoning the courage to investigate, I crept toward the door and was rewarded with the resounding thump, thump of a heavy tail from a dog who didn't mind being disturbed at dawn for a belly rub.

Our stay in Susa was delightful. Breakfasts served at the El Dorado were warm, sugary croissants filled with sweet apricot jam. Prosciutto slices with dried plums arrived at the same time as hot, frothy cappuccino, along with toasted sandwiches of thick ham and melted, dripping brie cheese. Hikes through mountains so high the tops were invisible in the mist. Church bells echoing in all directions from tiny chapels dotting the hillsides. The muted roar of the rushing stream – once we finally found it – became background noise for all outside activities. We followed a trail to a cascade towering thirty feet above us, the water thundering down so loudly all my exclamations of awe and wonder were drowned out. Cheryl found a smooth, dry rock to stretch out on and let the enormous power of the falls enfold her.

Our batteries recharged and our souls refreshed, we were ready to take on our biggest challenge so far – a rural Italian restaurant. We'd scoped out the Ristorante della Posta on one of our hikes and judging by the large number of cars parked there in the afternoon, we figured it had to be good. After our Viterbo restaurant escapade, we never went anywhere without our phrasebook and Italian to English food cheat sheet. Still, we were a bit nervous as we were seated and the waitress disappeared.

"Weren't we supposed to get menus?" I whispered.

"I thought so. But no one else is reading a menu either." We tried to be inconspicuous and watch other diners without looking either touristy or voyeuristic. The table was set with open bottles of both red and white wines and an assortment of bottled waters. Cheryl dug in bravely and poured us a glass of red. No one came running over to loudly berate us in Italian for breaking the rules, so we relaxed a little and enjoyed the fabulous wine. "This is their house brand, della Posta," Cheryl read from the label. If I could have bought a case, I would have, it was amazing.

Our waitress did reappear a few minutes later and asked if we were ready. At least that's what I thought she said. Cheryl and I exchanged confused looks, but we nodded yes, in hope of finally getting to see a menu. Perhaps this was just how it was done in this part of Italy. The waitress went from table to table asking the same question and was greeted with the same affirmative nods. We felt as though we had passed a major test.

Ten minutes later, out came the trays. Antipasti! With a huge platter of prosciutto and melon slices, she dished up two for each of us and then set off to the next table for the same. We had no idea what we were getting, but this was a fun way to do it.

"This is delicious! But I wonder what the main course will be?"

It turns out we had plenty of time to speculate. After the first tray was served, there were more – a total of five different antipasti! Carpaccio of beef with lemon juice, walnuts with hunks of fresh Parmesan, cream cheese with spicy sun-dried tomato paste, tuna slices with egg/mayonnaise topping, and finally stewed vegetables with eggplant, artichokes, and figs. It was incredible. As we were lamenting about how stuffed we were, our waitress came back; but with a pad and pencil this time. She was there to get our order for the "primi" or first course from a list tacked on the back of a door. Because it was in Italian, we'd missed it when it we came in. We thought we were finished and the meal was just beginning!

Choices for the primi were soups or pastas with vegetables, meat, or fish. I ordered the pappardelle with salmon and Cheryl had the tomato pasta. By the time our server came around to collect our dishes and take the "secondi" or second course order, we'd used our cheat sheet wisely.

"The secondi choices are roasted turkey, trout, beefsteak osso, formage, and a mistoof," Cheryl proudly translated.

"What's a mistoof?" I asked.

"Not sure," Cheryl said as she finished her primi with a sigh. "I'm so full I could burst, but I think I'll have the roast turkey."

I chose the trout and when we finally put down our forks, we were seriously worried about our ability to waddle back to the car. At that moment the attendant came by, produced clean plates and a menu for dessert. "I couldn't possibly eat another bite," I moaned as I pointed to a crostati with chocolate and amaretto. Cheryl picked a gelato trio of chocolate, vanilla and nutella. Absolutely delicious!

When the last plates were finally cleared, other diners around us started to pack up their things and leave. We still hadn't received a bill, so looked around for our server.

"Whatever the price, it was worth it." I said hopefully.

Cheryl agreed. "I'm sure it will be expensive, but every now and then we have to splurge. And this was a wonderful meal." She caught the eye of the lady who'd brought us all the amazing food and after pantomiming signing a check (or what we supposed was the universal sign for check please); she was given a piece of paper with two hash marks on it. No amounts, no total.

"I'll go up to the front desk and see what the charge is. Fingers crossed it won't break our budget."

I met her at the door, "I'm afraid to ask. How bad?"

"Well, for both of our meals, the wine and the water, the total was forty-four euros Total, tip included." She shook her head in amazement. "I would never in my life have believed such a fantastic meal could be had for that price."

Bellissimo Italy! With the bill gladly paid, we wobbled our way to the car, vowing to hike again as soon as we got to France. "Look! There it is again," I cried, pointing toward the white cross lit so brightly and sitting high on the mountainside. Susa was truly a magical place!

14

"The true traveler is he who goes on foot, and even then, he sits down a lot of the time."

- Colette

Bayonne, France

We're on our way to Spain! Woo Hoo!

We just have to get through the entire country of France first. Our first stay without pre-booking had been a success, so Cheryl was a little less apprehensive about taking our chances all through France.

"The tourist center here has Internet access. Would you feel better if we booked something on-line for the next few nights?" I asked after consulting a brochure in La Grave, where we'd stopped for lunch. "We can estimate being in Valence by tonight and Foix by the day after if we keep on schedule."

"No, it's okay. I'm starting to like this new and spontaneous Cheryl. I've always wanted to be more spur-of-the-moment and so far it's turned out pretty well." We were on such a high from the El Dorado in Susa. We should have known things could only go downhill from there.

La Grave, despite its creepy name, was the place we had our first look at Alpine snow. Hikers, bikers, and trekkers of all shapes and sizes were heading toward an incredible blue-white glacier tucked high up the mountain. The temperature had dropped so rapidly since we'd left Susa, we had to drag out layers of clothes from deep recesses in our backpacks before heading to lunch.

"Yuck, my jacket is one big wad and it stinks." I complained, tugging the remains of some unidentifiable foodstuff from a pocket.

"See, that's what happens when you hoard food. I remember one time at work you found a partial McDonalds cheeseburger in your purse. Gross!"

"I know, but it was all wrapped up. The cheeseburger was fine, a little on the hard side, but still edible. It's wrong to waste a perfectly good cheeseburger." I refused to be ashamed of my pack rat tendencies. I was secure in the knowledge she would be sorry for poking fun of me if we're ever stranded in the mountains without food, and I can produce a half-eaten Big Mac to share.

The drive through the French Alps was spectacular. And slow. Constant switchbacks, steep grades, and turtle-like speed limits pushed the limits of our little Peugeot. Rivers flowed by tinted the oddest shade of icy blue I'd ever seen. I wanted to rent a raft or a kayak and get in there, but judging from the temperature outside, I'd be as blue as the water in a few minutes time.

Briancon, one of the highest cities in Europe at 4300 feet, was in a state of massive growth and construction. Ski resorts and villages dotted the hills. There were bikers by the dozens at each intersection, ready to take on the mountains. The looks of sheer agony on their faces as they pedaled up the enormous inclines had me glad to be waving from the car.

"Look!" I shouted as we finally started our descent. "The bikers are coming down!" Behind us those tortured looks changed into maniacal grins. Pumping arms and shouts in every language sped past us as they took on the nine percent grade of a three kilometer downhill descent at wicked speed. They whizzed by us as though we were standing still, and the wild gleam in their eyes told the story of why they did this painfully exhilarating ride.

It had been a few days since we'd been on the Internet to check in with home, so I was anxious for us to find a place with Wi-Fi access to stay for the night.

In Valence. "Look," I pointed, "there's a place with Internet access. It's a Comfort Inn. I didn't know they had those in France. Let's stay there." Only after we'd checked in and lugged all our stuff into our sweltering room did we find the hotel's Wi-Fi had never been installed. Neither had air-conditioning. The only way to keep from melting into a puddle was to sit outside in garden chairs facing the busy roadside, praying for the wisp of a breeze.

In Foix. "I can't see the sign for the rain, but I think it says Wi-Fi." We swung into the packed parking lot of the Campanile and waited on a lull in the torrent. We'd hoped to arrive in Toulouse by evening, but the rain and fog had other ideas. The storm had been so bad, we opted to keep driving rather than stop for lunch. So right now even an old cheeseburger would have tasted good. "There's a restaurant here, too. We can get a late lunch and check out e-mail," Cheryl pointed out with as much enthusiasm as could be mustered after a nine hour drive.

Upon checking in dripping wet – there was no lull in the rain – we found the Internet was out and lunch service had finished a half-hour previously. No food would be available until seven PM.

"But there is a nice pub about five kilometers away in town, perhaps you'll find something there to eat?" The desk clerk added helpfully.

We were tired, wet and hungry – three things capable of bringing out my best qualities. "Fine," I grumbled. "Let's put our stuff in the room and go find food. I don't need to check my e-mail. For all I know a catastrophe could be going on back home and I wouldn't know anything about it."

"At least they have air-conditioning here," Cheryl said with a smile. I couldn't help but laugh, too. The rain had dropped the temperature in Foix close to what we'd experienced in the mountains. Here we felt a little out of place dressed in shorts, while everyone else was bundled in winter coats and parkas.

We found the pub easily enough. It was the only thing open in town at four in the afternoon. Imagining the taste of cheesy, noodley French comfort food, I eagerly ordered from the menu.

"Oh no," our server explained. "No food is served after three. Until dinner at seven."

"Not even an appetizer? A small bowl of onion soup?" I was almost in tears.

"Non, but you may have biere," she explained sweetly.

Two strong Leffe's later; we headed back to the hotel. The rain was still falling in sheets and I was certain I'd stashed a pack of cookies somewhere in my pack we could use to hold us over until dinner.

At our eight week mark of being on the road, we celebrated in Bayonne. As part of our celebration, we stayed at the beautiful Le Grande Best Western in the center of town. Here the Internet access was perfect. We were in heaven – or as close to heaven as we could through three solid days of torrential downpours.

It seemed we were the only people in Bayonne wearing shorts, except for a small group of schoolchildren we passed in the park. The rain-coated locals in heavy woolens we passed on the streets must have thought we were crazy. It felt perfectly comfortable to us, but to avoid being gawked at so frequently, we caved to peer pressure and zipped on the legs to our pants.

We saw the Cathedral of Notre Dame and admired Basque architecture in the mist. Learning the bayonet was invented here during the twelfth century whaling years added another useless fact to our ever-growing repertoire. We'd read the chocolate and jambon (ham) de Bayonne were not-to-be-missed; so we didn't. While the rain cleared the parks of tourists, we shared an afternoon admiring marble busts with only a bunch of wet pigeons for company.

"Why do they call it a bust?" I asked while shooing a pigeon from a dripping statue I wanted to photograph. I wanted a picture in case later I found time to look up the inscription to see who this famous person was. "I thought a bust was a woman's chest. I'm sure I don't know anyone who's well-known enough to have a bust made for them. Do you?"

Cheryl ignored me, watching the Adour River raging just a few feet away. Massive logs soared past at breakneck speeds as the rain-swollen river entertained us until the downpour forced us under shelter.

Our day trip to the Biarritz Surf Beach had to be put on hold until we could actually see the beach. The rain didn't show any signs of slowing, so we did what we do best. Found a warm, cozy pub and hunkered down for the afternoon. Lunch was the formule – a massive slice of lasagna, green salad, and carafe of vin du pays to wash it all down.

"Let's turn this into a working lunch," I offered as we sat down. "We should put together some thoughts on how we'd like to organize the *What Boundaries? Live Your Dream!* book."

"Sounds good. Let's make a table of contents first so we'll have a good outline of what needs to be covered." Cheryl added.

"Okay! I was thinking we'd start with our journals. Taking out snippets of places we'd visited. Maybe focusing on the journey and how we got here. Language, food, drink, customs, keeping in touch with those back home, laundry, learning…what do you think?" I took a quick breath, then launched on. "And when we've finished this book, we should look toward writing others about the volunteer expeditions we're going to in Mexico and Africa, and maybe one on the New Seven Wonders of the World. So, what do you think?"

Cheryl stared blankly at me with her pen poised over a notebook. "You lost me just after 'start with our journals'. I want to write all this down, but you're worse than all lanes converging on the Champs-Elysees. I need to focus on one area at a time."

It's a miracle we ever survived lunch, but after another carafe of vin, dessert, and café espresso, we managed to muddle through a rough table of contents and came a little closer to understanding what made each other tick on this trip.

Biarritz, France

It was as if the gates to Heaven had opened up. Sunshine poured through the windows and the bright blue sky blinded our cloud-shrouded eyes.

"What a beautiful morning," I exclaimed, jumping out of bed and running to the window to let my puckered skin soak up as much of the warmth as possible. "It's gorgeous here!"

"Too bad we're leaving today," Cheryl leaned out and took in deep breaths of the rain-cleansed air. It was the first time we'd seen the buildings in the sunshine, their colorful shutters shiny from the rain. We put this on our list of place we'd like to come back to in better weather, but today we were on our way to Madrid, with a planned stop in Biarritz as long as the weather held out.

The weather did hold and in just a few minutes we arrived at the famous Surf Beach. The famed lighthouse in the distance beckoned us closer. "What do you mean it's closed?" I yelped at the poor parking attendant simply trying to save us the cost of parking. "It can't be closed. We came to see the surfers."

It seems the recent storms had churned up the waters, so while there were a few people *on* the beach, no one was allowed in the water. Undaunted by the cold whipping wind, we grabbed sandwiches for lunch from a street side vendor and perched ourselves on the sea wall to breathe in the salty air.

"Look! Down on the beach – a couple is getting married." We watched as wind caught the bride's voluminous dress and turned her into a billowing white parachute. It was all the groom could do to keep her tethered to the sand.

"They're taking pictures." At least six photographers were snapping away at the beautiful, smiling couple from every angle. "Oh, no! The bride's getting too close to the water. She's going to destroy her gown!" I'm sure my running commentary was entertaining all English-speaking tourists within earshot.

It wasn't until the pair ran splashing into the surf we figured out this was a photo shoot and not an actual wedding. I'd never before witnessed two people ruining a wedding dress and tuxedo so totally. They propped on elbows in the sand as waves crashed over their backs, knelt over sandcastles as the water ebbed and flowed, and as the coup de grace, ran headlong into the water holding hands, disappearing in the surf. We were thoroughly entertained for over an hour.

"Ready to go?" Cheryl asked when it appeared our show was over.

"I'm ready. Can you imagine how happy those two will be to finally get those chilly wet clothes off and into something warmer? Brr!"

"Yes, but those are the hazards of modeling on Biarritz beach. Somebody has to do it." We fed our leftovers to the seagulls and piled back into the car, heading toward Madrid.

Madrid, Spain

"We're in Pamplona," I said excitedly when I woke up from my car nap. "This is where a man was gored by the bulls a few weeks ago. Let's go see it."

"See what? The place a man was gored?"

"No, to see the place where the bulls run."

"Do you know where that might be?" Cheryl asked.

"Not a clue, but I'm sure if we drive around, we'll find it." Sometimes my naiveté surprises even me. Pamplona is huge. Over 200,000 people occupy these narrow streets. The odds of finding the four I later learned to be Santo Domingo, Town Hall Square, Mercaderes, and Estafeta without a bull to guide us was slim. Still we drove around and enjoyed the chance to admire the city from the car.

"Would you ever want to come here for the San Fermin, Running of the Bulls, festival?" Cheryl asked.

"Not really. Getting gored by a bull isn't my idea of fun, no matter how huge the adrenaline rush is. And watching a bullfight doesn't interest me at all, Hemingway or not. But I did read about the 'Running of the Nudes' protesters do before the San Fermin festival. Now, that I would come back to see!"

Cheryl just shook her head, pretending to ignore me. Yet again.

We didn't quite make it to Madrid the first night. My naps kept interfering with proper navigation.

"Lisa, wake up. Are we going the right way? You said to stay on the highway, but with road construction we're going to have to take another route or we'll never get into Madrid."

I wiped the drool from my chin and consulted the map once again. "Let's head toward Zagora. Whoa, what are those?!" I'd never seen anything like what we'd just whizzed by. Giant robotic creatures surrounded us, covering the mountains in all directions.

"Aren't they cool? It's like driving through the set of a Star Wars movie." She could afford to be relaxed about these aliens; she'd had time to get used to gawking at them.

"Are they windmills?" I whispered as if the monsters could actually hear me. "The power they produce must be tremendous! And there are so many of them." I was in awe.

My respect grew as we now passed through huge fields of solar panels, moving in concert with the setting sun. "What an interesting crop. Solar power!" I later found out just one field of these mirrors produces enough power to give electricity to 6000 homes. Wow!

Our detour took us along the swollen banks of the river Bidasoa, where with the recent rains, the rushing waters threatened to cover the road. Equally frightening were the torrents of water cascading down the steep cliff side on the other side of the road. We were sandwiched between layers of water with nowhere else to go.

As the afternoon wore on, we decided to bag the idea of reaching Madrid before dark. Driving through a charming small town with the name of La Almunia de Dona Goddina, I piped up, "Hey, I've never stayed in a town with five names before. Let's stay here tonight."

After struggling with closed roads and potential rafting-by-car occurrences, Cheryl was more than happy to call it a day. We found a tiny kiosk in the town center with "Turissimo" written on the outside and practically scared the girl to death when we appeared at the door. From the look of the quiet town streets, we could be the only people she'd spoken within days.

Through a combination of pointing gestures, our bad Spanish and her passable English, we found the hotel she recommended. It was beautiful and the best part was their restaurant, El Patio de Goya. "If you are interested in having dinner with us, the restaurant opens tonight at nine," the desk clerk explained. Another Spanish custom we would have to get used to – thank goodness for afternoon tapas.

At 9:01, we presented ourselves to the hostess for seating. By eleven PM, we declared this to be the best meal we had eaten since starting this adventure. Cheryl had filet of beef medallions with mushrooms and I had filet slices with Iberico ham and truffles. For dessert, a glorious Crepe Suzette with chocolate mint glace to share. It was an amazing meal! We finished our coffee by eleven-thirty and the restaurant was still seating families with wide-awake small children. I was barely able to keep my eyes open and I'd taken a nice siesta. Spain was going to take a little getting used to.

"I can't believe we're lost again," Cheryl sighed. "We've passed this same intersection twice." Worried we might be overspending the travel budget with still a month to go, she'd booked us at another campground – Camping Alpha Bungalows just outside Madrid. Here we'd be close to the city, but have the capability to cook our own meals in the bungalow. And it was half the price of any hotel nearby.

Getting there was another challenge.

"Here are the directions again. Take A-4 12.400 to Madrid. Access entry Los Olivos to Quality Street number one," I read.

"We're on A-4. I just wish there was a sign." No sooner had she said this than an enormous statue of Jesus with his arms spread wide appeared on the hillside. About the same time, we spotted the Los Olivos access road and sure enough, the campground was in the valley below his outstretched arms. It wasn't exactly the sign we expected, but hey, we'd take it.

"Madrid has an Open Tour!" I chattered excitedly after unpacking our things. "We'll get to ride the bus again. I love the double-decker buses!"

"What did you put in your Diet Coke? You've got way too much energy."

I was just excited to be in Spain to see the capital city. This was another of the places on my Hemingway's-Been-Here checklists. This also was the home of the Prado with works by Goya and El Greco. Cervantes published Don Quixote here. Madrid has the most trees of any city in the world.

I'm ashamed to say one of our favorite stops on the entire Hop-On, Hop-Off Tour was TGI Friday's restaurant. We ate there twice. But even after we had our fill of American cheeseburgers and onion rings, I wanted to try the rioja alta from Casa Botin. I quoted the famous lines from *The Sun Also Rises;* "We lunched upstairs at Botin's. It is one of the best restaurants in the world. We had young suckling pig and drank rioja alta. Brett did not eat much. She never ate much. I ate a very big meal and drank three bottles of rioja alta."

"Do you know what rioja alta is?"

"It's a wine. I'm sure it's a red wine."

"Is Botin the only place in Madrid they serve rioja alta?" Cheryl asked. "We could probably order some at any restaurant close by and not have to find our way across town."

I had forgotten to note Botin's address before we set out, so we made a quick detour to a bookstore where the Madrid guides produced the location – quite a distance from where we were standing.

"Hemingway also mentioned Botin's in *Death in the Afternoon,*" I added helpfully.

"You want to visit a restaurant just because it was mentioned in two of Hemingway's books?" Cheryl asked.

"No, not only because of that," I said defensively. "Casa Botin is the oldest restaurant in the world. Goya worked there as a dishwasher when he was a teenager. Botin has history. Botin is famous."

Botin was closed.

We had walked for blocks. Passing through street after street of Spanish inspired architecture, adorable alleys with café's and shops, finally trotting down the steps of the plaza – and there it was! Empty and quiet. We asked one of the Madrillenos working close by and were told it closed two weeks every year for the family holiday.

"How can I find Papa's ghost if the restaurant he spoke so highly of is boarded up tight?" I lamented.

"Don't worry, there's always Barcelona." Cheryl said patiently. We'd traveled all over the world from Key West to Ketchum, then Paris to Spain, all in search of an elusive sentiment I craved – following in the footsteps of one of the greatest literary characters of all time. At least he was in my mind, anyway.

Cheryl didn't quite understand my obsession. "Why Hemingway?" she asked as we found a shady spot on the esplanade to rest. "Why not Virginia Woolf or Gertrude Stein? They were unique characters in their own right. Why him?"

"I'm not sure. I think it's because once I read the *Old Man and the Sea*, I fell in love with the simplicity and directness of his writing. How he bled each sentence down to its most basic parts. He suffered his craft and never seemed to think it was good enough; yet he also didn't take criticism well. But most of all, I admire him for not being afraid to be 'larger-than-life'. It's easy to hide behind words, but Hemingway lived life. I want to be like him!"

We sat for a while watching people and enjoying the glorious smell of magnolia blossoms mingling with roasted meats from street side vendors. Walking past the Prado and botanical gardens to catch our bus back to the campground, it was with true regret we left the beautiful city of Madrid – and Hemingway's Ghost – behind.

15

"Life is never going to be quite the same again after your passport has been stamped."

- Graham Greene

Valencia, Spain

"Oh, the sunflowers look so sad with their heads drooping." I noticed as we navigated rolling hills dotted with castles in disrepair and field upon field of drying sunflowers.

"My head is drooping today, too. Did we really drink a whole liter of limoncello last night?" Cheryl moaned. We did. And at the time it was wonderful. My new favorite drink in all Europe. So sweet and tangy, it was like we were sipping lemonade. Until we got up and tried to walk – wow, that stuff packed a punch.

With our pounding heads and limoncello hangovers in tow; we headed for Valencia. This would be our home base for the La Tomatina Festival in Bunol, scheduled for early the next day. Bunol was way too small for hotels; so Valencia, thirty-eight kilometers away, would be the closest train station.

"This is going to be so much fun," I crowed. "Thirty-six thousand people, one hundred forty tons of tomatoes, and us!" La Tomatina is labeled as the "biggest food fight in the world" and we were oddly eager to jump in to take our turn throwing ripe tomatoes at strangers.

"I read we should wear goggles. It will keep the tomato juice out of our eyes so we can throw more." Cheryl was getting a maniacal gleam in her eyes I had only noticed before when she was waiting for the gates at Disney to open. "Also, some people say to duct tape your shoes onto your feet because the streets get soupy after an hour of throwing."

"We only get to throw for an hour? Doesn't seem like very long."

"Just an hour. But the tomato throwing doesn't start until someone climbs a greased pole to pull down a ham. Once the ham falls, a horn blows, and the trucks start down the street. They toss tomatoes from the truck and then we toss them at each other. When it's over, the water cannons spray everyone down." Water cannons sounded wonderful about now. The August heat index was climbing to well over one hundred degrees.

"Let's go to Bunol first. I know we'll be taking the train there tomorrow, but I'd like to see what festivities are going on today," I suggested.

We found the tiny town without much difficulty. Stark, industrial, and bleak were my most favorable words to describe it. Quiet and sleepy, the only signs of what was in store for tomorrow were shopkeepers busily tacking up enormous sheets of plastic over window and doors.

"Look! He's putting up plastic over a third story window. Surely the tomatoes don't get tossed that high?" I wondered aloud.

A Bunol bicyclist stopped to gaze up with us. "You will be surprised," he said, shaking his head. "It's like nothing you have ever seen. You have goggles, yes?"

After cooling off with a huge draft beer at the Pardenvillas Bar, we headed back to Valencia to check in to our hotel for the night.

"Wow! This place is gorgeous," I gaped at the dizzying spiral staircase and thousand-watt chandelier of the Husa Reine Victoria.

Our room even came with a bidet! "Do you know how to use one of these?" I asked Cheryl before making a fool out of myself by flooding the entire room.

"No, but you can look it up on the Internet," Cheryl said from the desk, reading up on the logistics of our next day's adventure.

I came out of the bathroom twenty minutes later with a huge smile. I had mastered the bidet. I felt so thoroughly European.

"Did you know the back of your shirt is soaked?" Cheryl asked with a smile.

"Yes, I know. How kind of you to notice. I think I'm going to need just a little more practice with the bidet."

"You don't have much time to practice," she added with a grin. "We have to be out of here by 5:30 in the morning to catch our train for Bunol."

We were bleary-eyed the next morning, but ready for the tomatoes in our blindingly white t-shirts and shorts. Walking down quiet streets in pre-dawn Valencia, we wondered if we were heading in the right direction. Soon, however, the lights of the train station came into view and so did the scores of others already there waiting for the first train to leave at seven. I wedged myself between a man in a sequined wedding dress and another with nothing on except swim trunks, a mask, and snorkel.

When the train arrived, it was a mad crush of bodies to get on – standing room only. Costumed revelers in cow suits, Superman capes, and even a giant banana sang while the train wove its way through olive groves as the sun rose.

Goggles were a hot commodity on the streets of Valencia, but we'd heard they could be purchased at the festival. We needn't have worried. Many beer, duct tape, and goggle vendors were set up as we jumped from the train and followed the crowd in the direction of "The Ham".

A tall pole covered in several inches of white grease stood in the center of the plaza with "The Ham" tied on top. Shouts of "To The Ham" echo over the heads of the hundreds who were here before the first train arrived. Beers in hand and goggles atop heads, everyone waited in anticipation as the brave souls climbed over each other, standing on shoulders, and flinging great hunks of grease into the crowd. The costumed cow came close. I'm sure his udders gave a bit more traction than the shirtless men slipping down almost as fast as they could climb up.

It was a caped crusader with a bandit's mask who finally cut down the prize. The ensuing shouts from the crowds were nearly drowned out by horns and deafening blasts from the water cannons.

I took the first shot in the middle of my chest, staring in horror as the red stain expanded on my white shirt. I took a deep breath and realized I wasn't dying – La Tomatina was officially on!

Sounds of splats and scrunches combined with shouts of pure glee as adults of all shapes and sizes joined in a melee of ripe tomatoes and waves of icy water from the cannons.

"Hey!" I shouted as Cheryl squished a perfectly good tomato over my head. It was hard to make out features in all the goo, but I swore she was grinning like a fiend.

Thirty-six thousand people crammed into one-car streets intent on hurtling as many tomatoes as possible within the allotted hour. This is not for the faint of heart or those with claustrophobia issues.

At around the thirty-minute mark, the crowd started to move as one toward the water cannons. There were times when my feet were completely off the ground and I found myself chest to chest with bodies slippery with tomato gerb. I lost Cheryl in the crowd and just concentrated on not getting trampled into the street running heavy with tomato soup. Yelling to her was impossible. Heck, in the crush of bodies, breathing was impossible. It was like playing a game of rugby while standing calf-deep in gazpacho and abandoned flip-flops (now I understood the reason for the duct tape).

By the time the cannon sounded to end the throwing, I found Cheryl in a small alley away from the larger crowd.

"Oh my God! You are covered! Your clothes are totally red!" I panted, leaning on the wall breathing my first lung-full of air in the last half hour.

"You haven't seen yourself, yet! You're covered, too. I think you still have half a tomato on your head." She carefully picked the squished fruit from my matted hair.

Many locals, being the good sports they were, stepped from behind their plastic sheets to offer a running garden hose or bucket of water to grubby passer-bys. We stood under a balcony with a trickling water hose for a few minutes before we realized we'd require a lot more help to get these tomato guts from our body orifices. This time we followed the crowd to the Bunol River to clean up.

"The water is fr-freezing." I chattered, standing under the icy water as long as I could stand it, trying to dislodge slippery seeds from my hair and ears. I got off as much as possible to be passable for the train trip back to Valencia. We'd been warned the porters would not allow anyone on board looking tomatoey.

Our bodies dried quickly enough in the heat. As we savored a cold beer and the major accomplishment of not getting trampled, we were grinning from ear to ear. It was awesome. We had survived La Tomatina.

"Would you ever do this again?" Cheryl asked as we headed toward the train station.

"No way in hell," I replied, rubbing my already stiffening arm muscles.

"Me either," she agreed as we passed inspection and climbed on board our train back to Valencia.

For days we were reminded of our La Tomatina experience as we continued to find tomato seeds *everywhere*. You'd be surprised where those tiny seeds can go!

Barcelona, Spain

After La Tomatina, I swore wouldn't eat anything with a tomato in it for at least a week. I didn't want to look at anything red, squish or with those awful seeds I kept finding dried all over my body. However, the mussels marinara the couple sitting next to us was eating looked too good to miss. At the restaurant in L'Ametila de Mar, with a loaf of crunchy bread – this feast of garlicky, salty, and sweet flavors was worth breaking my word over.

"They call escargot 'winkles' here! Winkles, I love that name." I was in heaven. Soaking up the food and the charm of this tiny seaside town we'd happened upon on our way to Barcelona, we found pure bliss. With water an astonishing shade of blue and a vanilla glace with the taste of spun honey, what was there not to like?

Cheryl disappeared to use the restroom and came back, so proud of herself for communicating in Spanish. "It's the smallest restroom I've ever seen. But just as I was about to open the door, a Catalan gentleman pointed to the door and said 'bambino' and 'occupado'. I understood what he was saying!" she said excitedly. "In a few minutes, a little boy came out, not having locked the door behind him. I can imagine it would have been an embarrassing experience for all involved if I had walked in on him."

Communication notwithstanding, traveling around Spain was easy. We found our hostel in Barcelona on the first try.

"We found it! We found it!" I jumped up and down in my seat gleefully as we pulled up alongside the diagonal in front of the BCN Spot and found a place to park.

"This is a hostel?" I whispered as we taken past the dining room into the common area. The marble table could easily seat twelve. A balcony opened out to the street below and a welcome breeze cooled the room. If it weren't for the bunk beds in our room and the shared WC, I never would have believed we could stay here for fifty dollars a night.

Smells from the kitchen sent us out to the Supermercato to pillage our own food to cook for the evening. Finding an amazing bottle of Spanish wine for less than two euros was an added bonus. Sore muscles from La Tomatina made getting into the top bunk tough, but Cheryl insisted on taking it.

Barcelona became a place to rest and catch up while still experiencing all the city could offer two weary, achy travelers. Sitting outside in the Place del Sole, I was able to put down on paper all our major happenings since Madrid. I could imagine sitting out in this park for hours – a good thing because we'd accidentally left our laundry from La Tomatina in a plastic bag in the car. PU! We almost gagged when we opened the car door after it had been fermenting for a day. It was time to find a "lavanderie" and fast – extra hot and extra long cycles. The hostel directed us to the Place del Sole; full of sidewalk cafés, people tossing balls for their dogs, and a happy Lab puppy watching every move its master made in hopes she drops a crumb. The bigger dogs chase pigeons and little old ladies scold the furry rockets as they skid past.

"The pink and green confectioners' house looks like such an inviting place to live," I mused, more to myself than to Cheryl, who was deeply immersed in her own journal. The house had open windows with ceilings soaring to the sky. I listened as people around us chattered in Catalana dialects. The puppy yawned and much to my surprise, Cheryl pulled out *For Whom the Bell Tolls* to read. How appropriate!

I limp over to check on the laundry and it looks like our smelly clothes are going to need a second washing. Oh darn, we might have to order a second cerveza from the surly waiter who scowls at the customers, but stops to rub the puppy's ears on his way back inside. This is what I envisioned Europe to be. I could live right here.

Rested from our "day off" and with a nice stack of clean clothes, we were ready to explore Barcelona by bus. My mind was filled with names and places I'd only read about before.

"Let's splurge while we're here," Cheryl suggested. "We've been cooking our own meals at the hostel, so let's have a nice dinner out."

"And a Flamenco show?" I pounced eagerly.

"Sure, if you want. I've never seen Flamenco dancers, so this should be fun."

It was a blast! The frenzy of the music and the blur of synchronized movement were intoxicating. I wanted it to go on forever.

Walking back to our bus stop, we met a large crowd gathered expectantly around a multi-colored water fountain. "It's the Magic Fountain," I shrieked in excitement. "The Magic Fountain of Montjuïc!" And magic is was – a kaleidoscope of colors, music, and acrobatics of water so mesmerizing it held us spellbound. I had to purposely close my gaping mouth at times as the water came to life right in front of us. An amazing finish to the time we spent in glorious Barcelona.

Tomorrow we leave Spain and drive back across France, giving ourselves two days to make the trip to our next stop – Switzerland!

16

"People travel to faraway places to watch, in fascination, the kind of people they ignore at home."

- Dagobert D. Runes

Vouvery, Switzerland

"Today is September third. Labor Day holiday back home and no one knows it here," I sighed.

"That's because we're in France, on our way to Switzerland. Our Labor Day in the States means nothing here. Labor Day has never been a huge holiday for you to celebrate, has it?" Cheryl asked.

I'm not sure why it bothered me so much. The Fourth of July holiday we'd spent in Ireland hadn't felt so far from home, even though we'd missed the typical BBQs and gatherings at friends' houses then, too. But we cheerfully joined the celebration of Bastille Day in Paris, always eager to share an opportunity for a party. It wasn't the holiday I missed as much as it was the familiarity and comfort of friends and family.

"I guess it's because we've already been gone for nine weeks and as soon as we get back in October it will be time to pack for Mexico. And after that, ten weeks in South Africa. We'll be celebrating Thanksgiving out of the country and won't be back in the US for any length of time until next March. It's a long time." My sighs got deeper.

"You're homesick!" Cheryl cried. "Of the two of us, I thought you'd be the last to get homesick. You were so ready to go on this trip. What can I do to help?"

"Think we could find an Oscar Mayer hotdog to grill in France? With mustard?" I put on my best lost puppy face. I was homesick and the feeling surprised me even more than it did Cheryl. It had been over five months since I'd had an actual place to call home. Sadly enough, my home had always been integral to my self-esteem. It was a place I missed more than I'd realized – a place to feel comfortable in. I missed a refrigerator to pull out ingredients for a quick meal, without having to label my food while staying at hostels with my name and the dates we're leaving. I missed the simple pleasure of buying a small knick-knack to fit perfectly on the shelf back home.

My funk began to lift the second day of driving through France, as we arrived in Evian. I was sure a nice night in a hotel with Internet access to catch up with my peeps back home would be a sure cure. Huge Lake Lac Lemans beckoned to us, even with steel grey skies and crashing white caps. It was gorgeous. I envisioned shivering in our light jackets as we walked down to it from our hotel, then returning red-cheeked for some steamy hot chocolate in the lobby bar.

Our first stop to ask about a night's stay wasn't optimistic. "The hotel wants 300 Euro a night – for a 'town view'!" Cheryl yelped, jumping back into the car.

"But all the parking lots are empty. There's no one here," I whined. My bad mood was returning fast. The next hotel wasn't much better. Asking 150 Euros a night, they provided Internet service free for the first half hour, going up to seventeen euros an hour after that. With the Internet connections we'd been experiencing so far, I'd barely get signed on in a half hour. These prices were so far out of our budget, it was unbelievable.

We kept driving, staring wistfully as the lake disappeared behind us. Our reservations in Switzerland were for the following three days – at another campground. Unless we wanted to sleep in the car that night, it looked like I'd have to forget about the Internet and take the next place we found. Luckily, shortly after we crossed the border into Switzerland, we arrived in the picturesque "don't-blink-or-you'll-miss-it" town of Vouvery. Not only did the hotel have free Wi-Fi, but the gardens, birds, and mountain vistas surrounding us worked magic on my horrible mood.

Around eight pm, we were hungry and thinking our hotel served dinner, appeared downstairs to an empty room. Surprise! But they did direct us to a small restaurant down the hill. It was pouring rain, so we were the only people to occupy an enormous dining room. We were treated like royalty. The Gambas

Provincal was the best shrimp dish I've ever eaten. The buttery concoction of herbs and spices was so delicious I practically swooned. Cheryl had the beefsteak with an enormous bowl of au poivre sauce and pomme frites.

"I've decided to get over being homesick and get on with absorbing these beautiful places we're getting a chance to see," I told Cheryl as I dunked my bread in more buttery sauce. "If I miss having a garden in my back yard, I'll make the colorful produce in the farmer's market my garden. I can feel it and smell it without the hassles of bugs, grubs, or pesticides to worry about. If I miss the smell of dirt, I'll go on a hike and dig a hole. I'll watch tomatoes grow from the roadside in France. I won't confine it to four corners and a small patch of soil. The world will be my garden!"

Cheryl stared at me as though I'd lost my mind. "Where did all this talk about gardens come from? I didn't think you even liked vegetables."

Zweisimmen, Switzerland

"I've never used a window ledge as a refrigerator before," Cheryl remarked over my shoulder.

"Me either, but if want our beer to stay cold, this will work perfectly."

"Just don't drop it. I'd hate to get kicked out of this hotel because we dropped a Leffe on somebody's head. Besides, that would hurt," she added with a smile.

The Sport Hotel we were staying in certainly wasn't in our original plans. We had reservations at a campground in Juan Pass – up an incredible steep (but beautiful) mountain pass road. But because I read the directions wrong, we arrived at the campground twenty minutes after the reception closed at six.

"They can't be closed at six," I moaned, "it's a campground!"

Campground or not, they were closed tight. It was raining, windy, and about five degrees Celsius. I was colder than I'd been in a long time. We drove to two more hotels in Juan Pass – one was full and the other, you guessed it, Closed! This was getting tiring.

Spotting another open hotel on the way out of Juan Pass, we were sure this would be where we'd find a bed.

"Do you see anyone behind the desk," I asked as we walked through the door.

"No, but there's a bell. We'll just wait until someone comes back." Twenty minutes later, we came to the conclusion we were alone. No one was coming to the desk and even though we were warm and dry here; it would probably produce quite a surprise in the morning for the staff to find two women sleeping on their floor. It was time to strike out again into the elements.

By now it was close to eight, the temperature was dropping, and we were getting a bit worried. So when the Sport Hotel appeared, we gratefully took a room and only winced a little when we were told the exorbitant price.

"We're going to have to really watch our spending from now on," Cheryl said. "The trip budget is getting tight." I felt terrible. Because I was a dunce reading directions, we'd had to spend the same money for one night as it would have cost for three at the campground.

A quick visit to the grocery next door and at least we had Leffe's to chill on the window. The roar of a rushing stream drew us to look out until the biting cold forced us back inside to put on more clothes.

We took a short walk down to the stream and up a wooded path, but it was getting dark and we saw scary things around every curve. Every shadow seemed to turn into a living thing, waiting to lurch out at us as we passed.

"If the rain stays away, we'll go on a much longer hike tomorrow in the daylight," Cheryl promised.

Gstaad, Switzerland

"I think we've landed straight into heaven," I sighed sitting outside our chalet looking out over the mountains and gondolas. "If those darn falcons soaring by would just be quiet. Their shrill calls over the ridge are disturbing my meditation," I complained with a grin.

The chalet is gorgeous. And nestled happily in the refrigerator are the makings of a wonderful homemade dinner. Beef ragout from the butcher, a bottle of wine, fresh vegetables, soup stock, and potatoes – I'm gonna make a beef stew!

No, we weren't back at the campground in Juan Pass – we were in our own chalet at the foot of the mountain Reinecher. Serendipity at its best. From the Sport Motel that morning we hiked down to the thundering creek and back through the forest until we ran out of trail.

"There's a grocery in town," Cheryl suggested. "And further down the road is another trail to the cascade, what they call a waterfall here. We could pick up some food for a picnic lunch and see the waterfall here before we head to the campground."

The only parking available was in the lot of the Gstaad Tourism Office. On a whim, I grabbed a newsletter advertising chalet rentals from a box outside.

"Cheryl, look! This can't be right. See these prices?" She looked over my shoulder and without a word went inside the office. In ten minutes, the beautiful Swiss crew working inside printed up a list of chalets available for rent – all at prices considerably less expensive than the campground at Juan Pass. How could we pass this up?

"We tried to phone the lady who owns the one you want, but she's not in right now," the blond ski instructor explained. "If you will come back at two, when we reopen from lunch, we will call again for you."

Darn, this meant we'd have to do another one of those amazing hikes through the glorious Swiss Alps.

"I love Switzerland," I gushed as we parked behind a stream leading to a rumbling waterfall high above our heads. "The people are so friendly and proud of their country."

"And why not?" Cheryl added. "There is so much beauty here. Towns with the charm of a storybook. Swiss chalets, sweet children, and mountains so majestic they make you want to cry."

I nodded, but it was hard to continue a conversation as the trail we were climbing went straight up. And up. Then up some more. The steep slants opened to snow-capped mountain vistas that literally stopped us in our tracks. The sound of chainsaws drifted up from the village below as they prepared for the rapidly approaching winter. Buzzing saws melded nicely with the birdsong as we climbed.

We found a perfect place to stop for lunch along the trail. On one side, green fields dotted with yellow wildflowers stretched for miles. On the other side, a forest thick with growth allowed no sunlight to seep through its cover. We plopped down on the still-damp grass and had our feast of ham and turkey on homemade hot cross buns.

"You know," Cheryl mused, "I think this is the finest view of any restaurant I've ever been to before." Below us in the village, sweetly decorated houses posed postcard-perfect at the foot of the Swiss Alps.

When we returned to the Tourism Office, we were greeted by smiles and printed directions on how to find our new home for the next three days. As we drove into the driveway and unpacked our bags, we kept shaking our heads in wonder. Petunias threatened to spill out of window boxes, butterflies teased, and the resident feline was already stretched sunning on the Willkommen! mat. This was an incredible find.

Later that evening, with our stomachs full of homemade beef stew (the best I've ever made!); we watched in awe as the lights of the town below us began to wink on. And as night drew its cloak tighter around us, the sky began to bloom with sparkles. So many stars it was impossible to comprehend the grandeur of the enormous space in front of us.

A tiny light moved with precision along the hillside. "What's that?" I whispered, not wanting to break the reverie of such a spectacular show.

"It's a train. Moving up the mountain. Taking people to the other side."

We watched until the cold forced us back inside. My teeth were chattering, but I didn't want the night to end. Back inside, we talked about how neither of us wanted to go back to the lives we knew before. Was there a way to incorporate travel into writing full time? Since we were already signed up to volunteer globally in Mexico and South Africa, what about possibilities of volunteering across America? Could we make our adventure something others could use to follow their own dreams?

We woke to a thick layer of frost on the chalet and our laundry held hostage. The night before Cheryl tossed everything we owned in the shared washer, measured detergent, and then slammed the door. Nothing happened. No buttons would push. We even checked the electric plug and everything looked as though it should work – but it didn't. Cheryl tried to take the clothes out, but the glass door was locked tight. We could see them in there, but not being sure what ransom was required, we couldn't get them out. Lucky for us, the lady who owned the chalet came by to check on us that morning and produced a card to swipe. If she hadn't made her rounds when she did, we'd had been completely out of underwear – not a good thing at all!

Vaduz, Liechtenstein

"Did you know the entire principality of Liechtenstein is only sixty-one square miles? The whole country?" I read from the Atlas Fun Facts. "Oh, and it's the world's largest producer of dentures!"

"My junior high school geography teacher used to talk about this place all the time. I'll have to e-mail him and let him know I was there."

"If we can ever find it," I muttered under my breath.

"I heard that," Cheryl said. "I know it was my idea to stay here, but I didn't count on how long it would take us to drive through the mountains from Gstaad."

It hadn't been a long drive in terms of miles, but traveling through several mountain passes, hundreds of switchbacks, one or two photo shoots, and a snowball fight had eked the hours out of the day.

At seven PM, we made a first pass through Vaduz, the capital of this sixth smallest country. "Only 35,000 people live here and I'll bet ninety-five percent of those are out either hiking or alpine trekking. These must be the healthiest people on earth," I stared as people walked by with trekking poles, dressed in business suits, lederhosen or delightful argyle sweaters and knickers.

We'd made reservations at a hostel in Vaduz, but after our fifth pass through the tiny town it became apparent finding it wasn't as easy as we'd hoped. No one we asked could point us in the right direction.

During the last few days in Gstaad, we'd hiked and biked more than we'd done in months. Three glorious days of soaking up vistas, racking up miles, and enjoying the friendly people. But now sore muscles and worn out psyches don't fit well with being lost. By eight, we gave up and parked at the expensive-looking Hotel Engle.

"One hundred fifty euros a night?" Cheryl cried to the reception, while I tried not to cry in the corner. I was exhausted and even the thought of depleting our travel account to fumes wasn't enough to turn me away.

A bottle of wine we'd brought with us kept us sane and by the time it was finished, we were almost too worn out to enjoy the fluffy down comforter and soft beds that awaited us. Almost.

"Hey, look at this," I announced the next morning, proudly showing Cheryl my ability to now zip up my vest with a bulky sweater on underneath. "Before we started this trip, I couldn't zip it up at all. Now look."

She agreed this was quite a milestone as we went downstairs in search of a hearty breakfast. Bacon, anyone?

St. Anton, Austria

"You know what this Sunday is, don't you?" I asked sadly as we drove toward Innsbruck, Austria.

"I know. It's Football Sunday. Football season officially starts tomorrow," Cheryl said with a sigh. "It's the first year I have season tickets for the Buccaneers and the first time we'll be so far away there's no chance to see any of the games."

The melancholy in the car was palpable. Both of us are huge football fans, so missing out on opening weekend was akin to finding out your long-awaited vacation flight canceled due to a hurricane.

As the afternoon shadows lengthened, I picked a small town from the map as we neared Innsbruck. "Let's try our luck at St. Anton. It's at the foot of the mountains and not too big."

We stopped at an information booth by the road – no one manning it this time, but lots of listings of apartments and hotels in the area. While we were stomping in the cold trying to figure out how we'd know the prices, a gentlemen sitting in his car came out and handed us a booklet with everything listed by price. He was a Godsend.

Cheryl picked a place that looked nice. Haus Pirker advertised reasonable apartments with their own kitchenette and a LAN line for the Internet. We found the address, but the town looked absolutely dead. Not a soul in sight. We almost walked away, but Cheryl bravely rang the bell again while I waited by the car.

Finally, the door was opened by Jugen, the nice man of the house we'd interrupted from his own Saturday afternoon of sports. He showed us to our gorgeous apartment with a view of the town from one window and a mountain waterfall from the other.

It was beautiful. And the best part? Once we connected to the Internet, we found Yahoo provided an NFL Pass to those not living in the States. We could see ALL of the games through the computer! We were like college kids, buying beer and chips at the only open store in town – the gas station – in anticipation of tomorrow's games. For now, though, it was time to explore this corner of Austria.

"You know, I can't imagine how journal writing could be in much better than this," Cheryl sighed, sitting high above the village of St. Anton. Below us, the river is coursing through the center of town, icy white and rushing fast. The sky is a crystal shade of blue that makes the snow-capped mountains ping out in 3D relief. Ski lifts busily ferry summer trekkers up the mountain for a heavenly view.

We were taking a short rest after petting horses and cows, getting our fingers sticky from sweet, pine-scented sap, and hiking through the forest while the sound of a nearby waterfall pounded our ears.

"This is so different from the way we started," Cheryl observed. "Here we're not looking for museums, monuments, or tour buses. We're looking for those places we can feel nature and just take in all the beauty she has to offer."

While we thoroughly enjoyed the cities like Paris, Rome, or Madrid; they are quite touristy. In St. Anton we could surround ourselves with soaring mountains and the smell of fresh fir trees, accented by a roaring waterfall. It was an outdoor paradise.

Dorle, at Haus Pirker, took such good care of us. Each morning she would go to the market to buy fresh rolls and the sweetest apricot jam I've ever tasted. Staying in their Haus felt like home, especially when we were able to catch Sunday football games.

"You realize we're six hours behind here," Cheryl explained. "The game normally on at one pm isn't on here until seven. And the four pm game won't start until ten."

"It's okay with me," I said with a grin. "As long as we can see football, I'm not afraid of a long night."

Our last day in St. Anton, we decided to enjoy the outdoors as much as possible. We'd found a pasture nearby where the most beautiful horses were grazing. Honey-golden with a white-blond mane and tail, these Haflingers were spectacular and I was smitten.

"Thank you for cutting up the apples," I said to Cheryl when she finished stuffing them into a plastic bag. All morning I'd been talking about bringing a treat to those beautiful creatures. It had been raining all day, but the afternoon cleared in time for us to go find my horses.

The herd wasn't at their normal spot down by the fence, but way up on the hill.

"Can we get to them?" I asked.

Trying to avoid my disappointed pout as much as possible, Cheryl suggested we take one of the cross country ski paths up the mountain. The ground was so mucky from the rain, it was difficult to tell where the mud ended and the cow patties began. It was a steep, slippery climb and Cheryl started to regret it as soon as we leveled off.

"Do you realize we're in the middle of a field with cows as well as your horses?" She commented with growing concern. "The cows have huge horns, too. Did I ever tell you about the time I was chased by a cow? I'm still afraid of them. And these have huge horns. We should go back before they realize we're here," she turned to slide back down the hill.

It was a little late for a quick escape as the one of the horses had spotted us and was ambling our way. I was ecstatic. I'd get to feed one of them apples, after all. A gorgeous mare with a wide blaze, gently took the apple from my hand with the softest lips. I even had time to rub her ears before the stampede began. In just seconds, I was surrounded by eight or ten – it felt like fifty – very muscular, wild animals all intent in getting their share of what was in the bag I was carrying. While incredibly gentle with me when I offered my hand, they were not so kind to the others in the herd – kicking, butting, biting, and pushing each other out of the way. They jockeyed for apple position and I was right in the center of it. As I disappeared between mountains of kicking horseflesh, I yelled to Cheryl for help.

"They're going to trample me!" I shouted over their whinnies. "I can't get away. Help me! Help me, please!"

She wasn't getting anywhere near me, but did yell advice in my direction. "Drop the bag! Drop the bag!"

When one of the horses moved in the direction of the bag, I could see her standing there, snapping pictures and laughing hysterically. Here I was being attacked by wild horses and she was taking pictures!

I ran away while tossing the last apple slices in the direction of the herd, terrified to hear hoof beats bearing down on me as I slipped and slid behind a tree. I could still hear Cheryl laughing as I peeked my head around the trunk.

"Are they gone?" I panted.

"No, but they aren't chasing you anymore," she hooted. "They're grazing. You can come out now."

As we picked our way back down the mountain, covered in black mud or worse; we kept looking behind us – Cheryl for the horned cows and me for the stampeding horses. When we were back on the road, I looked up at the calm clan of horses quietly grazing.

"I think I'll enjoy them from a distance the next time," I said, wiping bits of apple and horse gerb from my hair.

"Oh no," Cheryl chuckled. "This was the most fun yet! I've never laughed so hard in my life. And I've got the pictures to prove it!"

17

"When the journey's over there'll be time enough to sleep."

- A.E. Housman

Bad Gastein, Austria

"What's a perlzweibel?" I asked while perusing the menu at Wasserfall Park. We'd been hiking for nearly three hours and it was time to find sustenance. In my case, sustenance would be in the form of a pizza – if I could just figure out what the ingredients were. "I think I know what mais is, though why anyone would want corn on their pizza is beyond me."

"I'm going with tomatoes, kase, salami, and speck," Cheryl said. "Your basic meat and cheese pizza." Our voices were slightly louder than normal to be heard over the thundering roar of the Bad Gastein Wasserfall, tumbling over a thousand feet and so close we could feel the spray from our table.

While in Vaduz, a bit of serendipity led us to pick up a copy of a European backpacker and hostel magazine advertising a place in Austria called Bad Gastein. "How can we not stay in a place with a name like that?" I asked, reading more about it out loud. "Bad means baths. Thermal baths. And it says 'the village is a Mecca for outdoor enthusiasts with hiking, biking, white water rafting, and paragliding as summer sports'. What do you think?"

"Hmm…thermal baths would feel good after a long day of hiking through Alpine forests. I'm game if you are!"

"The Hotel Krone Hostel is offering a free night if you pay for four. And the prices are already low. That's a great deal!" I was getting excited just reading about it. I was in love with the outdoors of Austria already and the thought of spending more time exploring it put me close to heaven.

Driving through the snow-capped panoramas of Austria was a breathtaking experience. When we arrived at the town of Bad Gastein and found the Euro Youth Hotel and Krone, I thought we'd found paradise. Dating from the mid-1880's, this delightful old hotel (facing a ski slope affectionately referred to as "Stairway to Heaven") had been recently converted into a hostel. The rooms were huge and faced the mountain with a view I couldn't stop gaping at. But one of my favorite highlights we found on our way out to explore.

"I smell food," I bloodhound sniffed as we came down the stairs. "What's in that room back there?"

We peeked in and adding to our total happiness; there was a gorgeous bar and restaurant, right on the premises. It wasn't open until later, but the menu promised Austrian delights and beers from Munchen (Munich). "It can't get much better than this," I said with a grin.

But it did. The town of Bad Gastein was truly one of those straight-out-of-the-storybook places. Huge evergreens, so big they seem to grow into the sky – the bluest I've ever seen, so cloudless and clear. The Wasserfall is a centerpiece to the town and the roar becomes a welcome background noise; soothing, like the quiet of soft pine needles underfoot in the forest. Trails winding up and around the mountains surprise us at how far we've come when the vista opens up and the entire town spreads out below. We felt as though we'd earned the pizza and beer at Wasserfall Park – and the perlzweibel? Those were flawless pearl onions, complimenting the pizza perfectly!

That evening we relaxed on our balcony overlooking the glorious Gastein mountains. The train tracks in view sang as they brought in weekend visitors, bundled in heavy coats and carrying trekking poles with their luggage.

"I can't believe we found the exact wine we love so much at home in a little grocery here for only three euros!" I mused, admiring the four bottles chilling on the balcony. Our muscles were sore from the long climb, but we were ready for another day of exploring.

"So, would you like to rent mountain bikes tomorrow? " Cheryl asked while mapping our route in a different direction from where we'd gone today.

"Sounds good! Where are we going?"

"According to this ski map, the town of Sportgastein is not very far away. There are marked trails directly from the bicycle rental. Let's head there."

I was all over it, packing our daypacks with all the essentials for a day on a mountain bike. "I've got rolls, turkey, olive loaf, and I replaced the yucky wine-in-a-box with some of the Grand Sud from last night. Oh, and two plastic cups, too."

"I guess I'll be in charge of the water. If you think we have room for it."

I looked up in time to notice the sarcasm and rolled eyes, but didn't care. If I was going to be exerting myself in the mountains, then I wanted a proper picnic when we were finished.

"So you ladies are experienced mountain bikers, eh?" the boy behind the bike rental counter asked the next morning as we filled out the paperwork.

"We both ride back in the States. But it's been a while. Why?" I asked, little alarm bells starting to ring in my head.

"Well, you said you were heading to Sportgastein. It's a trek," he said slowly.

"How far is it?" Cheryl asked.

"About nine kilometers," he said solemnly. We looked at each other and smiled. Under six miles, that was nothing. We regularly rode twenty or thirty miles back home with no problem. For six miles, we'd be there and back before noon.

He shrugged and showed us how to lock the bikes properly. "If you fancy a stop along the way, I can show you a good place." We readily agreed. When locals offered you a recommendation, it was usually a good idea to take it. He marked a spot on our trail map with an X. "If you stop here, be sure to order the Zirbenschnaps."

Noting smirks from the other guys working in the shop, Cheryl asked for more information. "What is Zirbenschnaps? And how do you spell it?"

Our guy just smiled, shrugged, and wrote down the spelling on the map. "Try it," he suggested, "then let me know what you think."

With bikes under us and packs stuffed with goodies on our backs, we headed toward Sportgastein. The first two miles were absolute bliss. Meadows of wildflowers backed by steep, rocky cliffs lined our path on one side. Waterfalls trickled and plunged to form a roaring stream of icy blue on our other side. Sleek horses stood by the fence, looking longingly at our backpacks as we pedaled by. Cheryl made some comment about horses and apples as we passed, but I pretended not to hear her chuckling.

The picturesque parish church of Bockstein, built in 1766, was letting out services as we passed. Cheryl filled her water bottle from an icy fountain. A gentleman with a scarf sat at the foot of the hill with his sketchbook and paints, absorbing the brilliant fall colors.

Once through Bockstein, the path began to climb. And climb. And climb. Soon it was so steep, we had to get off the bikes and push them. Each step became a huge chore. While the scenery around us was spectacular, it was hard to enjoy it through all of the panting and puffing we were doing just to keep forward momentum.

"I…had…no…idea," I wheezed as we continued up the slope. We found others following the same path, but instead of cumbersome bicycles, these smart people were leaning into stout trekking poles to help them make the climb.

Cheryl sat down beside me, breathing heavily. "Nice place to stop. The view is amazing."

I didn't notice. I was too busy gasping for air. "We still have four miles to go. I'm not sure I'll make it."

When my face was a little less red from exertion and passing out wasn't imminent, she suggested, "Why don't we try a little further? The place the boys marked on the map shouldn't be too far. I know you want to try a Zirbenschnaps. That'll make us feel better."

Before we left our perch, a group of three hikers met up with us and asked to share our seat. They were from Munich on a short holiday to enjoy the mountains. "We'll see you on the trail," I said as we continued on, using our bikes like rolling crutches.

It felt like hours of climbing before we spotted Astenalm, an oasis in the Alpine forest. "It's our schnapps stop," I cried happily, relishing the feeling of pushing my bike downhill to the outdoor seats. We had stumbled upon an inn and restaurant it seemed time had forgot. A working farm, Astenalm's specialties were fresh butter, cheese, and speck (bacon). However, we were here in search of schnapps.

Before we had a chance to order, we were visited by two friendly goats with clanging cowbells, nuzzling for food.

"Something just bit my foot," Cheryl yelped. I looked under the picnic table and saw the culprits – a kindergarten class of ducklings, tugging at her shoelaces. A feisty kitten joined the fray and soon the entire menagerie moved off to visit other tables of hikers (crazies) like ourselves who were trying to master a mountain.

Our new friends from Munich soon appeared at the end of the driveway, and with all the seats now taken, we motioned for them to join us at ours.

"It's amazing how a morning out in the fresh air can whet an appetite," I remarked as we ordered our Zirbenschnaps.

"You've tried this schnapps before?" the gentleman asked with raised eyebrows.

"No, actually we were told to try it by the boys at the bike shop. What is it?" Cheryl asked.

"Try it, and then let me know what you think," he said with a wicked smile.

"Funny, that's exactly what they said back in Bad Gastein," I added.

The glasses arrived at our table and with all eyes on us, we tipped them back. I gasped and swallowed. Cheryl's eyes teared a bit as she set the glass down with a bang on the table.

"Wow, that was strong!" was all she managed. I wasn't able to speak for a few more seconds.

"You girls did well," our companion said with a grin. "Zirbenschnaps is an acquired taste and it takes some people all their lives to acquire a taste for it. It's made from the fruit of Christmas trees growing high up on the mountains. It's strong, but tasty," he said as he ordered another round for everyone at the table.

Their food arrived shortly afterward – a tray of assorted farm goodies, breads, and cheeses. He picked up a slice of brown bread, spread it thickly with an unidentifiable meat paste – and to Cheryl's horror – handed it to her.

"Thank you. Um, what is this?" Her face had decidedly gone a shade paler. Being daring with a tiny taste of pate in France was one thing, but she wasn't about to try this funny looking stuff on a hillside in Austria.

"It's verhackeles," he said with a mouth full. "It's delicious."

Caught like a deer in the headlights, Cheryl did the only thing possible to save herself from appearing rude. She quickly handed half of the bread to me.

"Here, you should try this," she smiled sweetly, practically tossing it in my lap.

"What exactly is verhackeles?" I asked before taking the bread from her. I was enjoying watching her squirm way too much. I wasn't sure of proper pronunciation or spelling of this new food, but must have come close because he knew what I was asking.

"The best way to describe it would be speck tartare," he replied. Hmm, raw bacon. Interesting. As they watched, we swallowed with a smile and happily finished our glass of Zirbenschnaps to wash the rest down. I asked Cheryl later what she thought. "The consistency was a little odd. And the USDA might not approve of it, but it went well with the schnapps." Anyway, we survived.

The trip back down the mountain to Bad Gastein was a blast. We rode the bikes this time, streaking past laboring hikers with huge grins on our faces. When we finally pulled into the bike shop to return our mode of transportation for the day, we couldn't wait to tell the boys we'd tried the Zirbenschnaps. They were most appreciative of our efforts and told us to be sure not to miss the Harvest Festival in the next few days.

"Everyone sells schnapps there. You can try many different kinds. The parade starts at one o'clock." We were stoked. An Austrian Harvest Parade and schnapps – a great combination.

Our dinners in Bad Gastein became a 'what schnitzel tonight?' game. We enjoyed Weiner Schnitzel and Gebackenes Putenschnitzel at the Krone. For a change, we tried Devil Schnitzel at a small inn along the trail. By the third night, we were tossing around ideas again.

"So far, on this trip we've eaten authentic Thai, Chinese, Indian, Irish, Italian, French, Belgian, German, and Spanish foods," I ticked off on my fingers. "What haven't we had yet?"

"Mexican!" Cheryl piped. "We haven't had Mexican food and I could use a nice margarita after all the hiking and biking we've been doing."

So began our search for Mexican food. In small town Austria. The girl working behind the desk at the Krone suggested a popular place just by Wasserfall Park downtown. About a twenty minute walk from the hostel, it sounded like just what we were looking for. Sombreros hung from the ceiling and the sound of a blender churning out margaritas turned Cheryl's head as soon as we walked through the door. We ordered the *Mexican Special for Two* and our *jaws* dropped at the amount of food brought to the table. Filets of steak, chicken, and pork piled high on top of tacos, chili con carne, spare ribs, chicken wings, fresh corn on the cob, grilled veggies, and roasted potatoes – it was a Mexican mountain of food! Thank goodness for the walk back home or we'd have been in no shape for the Harvest Parade the next day.

From our balcony we watched the parade set up as tractors and wagons passed by, honking and cheering, filled with lederhosen-clad gents and ladies in long, fitted dresses.

"Look!" I pointed from the window. "More goats. They must be a big part of the parade."

"Or maybe the schnitzel served afterward," Cheryl pointed out helpfully.

It was time to go join the festivities. As soon as we walked outside the door, we were met by two frauliens – one with a cask slung over her shoulder and the other with a basket full of glasses. They were selling schnapps! They poured us two and watched as we slammed them down.

"Oh my God!" I sputtered, "that's horrible!"

It burned all the way down, but from the nods and smiles of the ladies selling it, mine was a typical reaction. Of course there was no way to wash the glass after a person drank, so they used a well-worn kitchen towel to wipe it off each time.

On our way to find a spot to watch the parade, another two young ladies met us, begging us to try "their" brand of schnapps. "Surely it can't be as bad as before?" I said hopefully, while parting with another euro in exchange for a glass.

It was just as bad. Maybe worse. But by now, the chilly day didn't seem so cold.

The parade was exactly as I'd have expected an Austrian Harvest Festival to be. There were logging demonstrations, children with pet calves, flowers and hay bales, and my favorite – the sooted chimney sweeps. The crew would jump from their truck and run into the crowd, giving big kisses (and cheeks of soot) to the women in the crowd. I wore my blackened face with pride the whole afternoon; though there were several times I got quite a fright when passing a mirror.

Freistadt, Austria

Some of the places we landed for one night could best be described as "one night blunders". It could be that the hotel shower wouldn't work, our phone would ring all night, or the room came with bars on the windows to discourage guests from leaving without paying. However, our ending up in Freistadt, Austria proved to be a most welcome "one night wonder".

Our reservations in Prague were rapidly approaching. The extra night we'd stayed in Bad Gastein only gave us one night to drive through the mountains to the Czech Republic and we weren't sure exactly what we'd find along the way.

A cold rain started a few hours into our drive and we both were feeling a little sniffly and grouchy. For some odd reason, I navigated us across the German border twice that day. The second time we were greeted to a full military-style roadblock. Soldiers sauntered over to our packed little Peugeot and carefully looked through our stuff as though we were transporting mass quantities of illegal limoncello. One rough-looking fighter even pushed the barrel of his gun through the window as his cohort looked over our passports.

"What's going on?" I whispered as we rolled through the gauntlet of soldiers.

"I have no idea," she whispered back, looking straight ahead. "Any time we've crossed the borders before we've just been waved through."

Several long minutes later we came upon a large convoy of what-looked-like-missiles stopped by the side of the road. They were huge and scary. We couldn't wait to get back into Austria with our secret limoncello stash.

Pulling into the Hauptplatz (town square) of such a charming place as Freistadt helped lift our spirits, even in the pouring rain. The visitor's center was brightly lit and invitingly warm and dry inside.

"Would you be looking for a hotel or a pension for the night?" the helpful lady behind the desk asked.

Cheryl and I looked at each other. We'd mastered singles, doubles, dorm rooms, and shared baths, but a pension was a new term for us.

"Um, what is a pension?" Cheryl asked.

"A pension is a guesthouse. There you'll have a room including home-cooked breakfast." A home-cooked breakfast sounded really good. And the price for the guesthouse pension was significantly less expensive than the local hotel. With directions in hand we drove out of the city gates – then back inside again – to find the Pension Pirklbauer set directly against the twelfth century walls surrounding this charming village.

"It's gorgeous," I whispered as we admired the glorious bundles of flowers hanging from windows boxes and planted in enormous vases inside. The smell of fresh petals was intoxicating.

The lady of the house showed us to a beautifully furnished room with pickled oak paneling and a sitting area overlooking the outside garden. I looked in envy at the wrought iron chairs and lanterns on the deck; but even through the cold drizzle, the view was grand.

It was only our grumbling stomachs and the threat of approaching darkness that roused us from the warm, dry comfort of our room and into the elements outside. Construction was being done in the square, so the first time around we missed the lights of the only open restaurant in town. Just as we resigned ourselves to going back to the room – cold, wet, and without dinner – we ducked behind some scaffolding to find a welcoming glow beckoning inside. There was only one other couple sitting down, but the smells were heavenly.

"Can you read the menu?" I asked Cheryl, while discreetly blowing my nose.

"It's in German. Or a mixture of Austrian and German," she replied, gently shaking water out of her hair.

Our waiter came over and after apologizing profusely for not having an English version of their menu, proceeded to explain it to us completely. He was such a delight! We decided on pork cordon bleu – stuffed with spinach and speck for me; spinach, ham, and mozzarella for Cheryl. This masterpiece was breaded in a pumpkin seed mixture, lightly fried and came with potatoes and currant compote that set the flavors perfectly. It was absolutely delicious.

Once we finished this feast, we were far too full for dessert, but our waiter suggested schnapps as a digestive and to brace ourselves for the walk back to our pension. He gave us several flavors to choose from and we settled on the apricot. The smell? Glorious! The taste? Awful! But it did warm us up a bit so the walk in the dark along the ancient and looming city walls wasn't quite so frightening.

"This feels surreal," I murmured as we passed gates built over nine hundred years ago. The village church dedicated to St. Catherine held the highest point in Freistadt since the fourteenth century. I could imagine the bustle and smells from the medieval days when this was the center of the iron and salt trade route from the Danube to Bohemia. Here it felt as though we were taking giant steps backwards through history.

Before heading to Prague the next day, we forced ourselves out into the freezing (but sunny) air to explore this charming parish. My favorite was the choir of St. Catherine's – playful angels playing musical instruments hung all along the choir wall. It brought welcome smiles to two feverish and sniffling travelers.

Prague, Czech Republic

"It's not really called the Prague Pillow, is it?" I asked, stifling a sneeze. "And where are the directions?"

"Everything written on the web site is what's written on the paper," Cheryl sighed as the morning melted into early afternoon. "There was only an address for the Prague Pillow Hostel, no directions. We'll have to stop as we get closer to find Internet access to get a real address." Poor thing, she was feeling awful, too.

There was only one thing we could do.

"Let's pull off at this exit," I suggested. The Golden Arches called to us with a Siren's Song of comfort food – a cheeseburger to fill the stomach and a milkshake to soothe our sore throats. And free Internet Wi-Fi to help us toward our next destination.

We pulled into the city limits of Praha (Prague) a few hours later. Hopelessly lost, but buoyed by the medicinal sugar level of a McDonald's vanilla shake.

"We need a better map. This one doesn't get down to street level," I observed, trying to match up our directions with what the atlas provided.

"There's a mall," Cheryl cried. "A real mall. We haven't seen one of those in weeks."

We gaped at the brightly lit neon and drooled a bit at the smell of fresh popcorn wafting from the cinema. The bookstore provided a detailed street map of Prague in English with the only hitch being we were forced to switch to Crowns for payment because the country didn't yet accept euros.

"Look at this. The mall is here. The road the Prague Pillow is on is here. We're only a couple of blocks away!" I was practically giddy with excitement. Someone was looking out for us.

Our room at the hostel looked out over the courtyard. Excellent for both charming views and acoustics from travelers who came out every evening to play instruments until four AM. I learned at least five language variations of old favorites like *Start Me Up and Proud Mary*. They sounded as though they were having lots of fun, but with both of us sick; I was soon over all the fun.

It was in Prague that we hit the wall. The first full day of sightseeing had us up early to catch the tram into the center of the city. We jumped on board and looked around for someone or something to pay our money. No one seemed concerned. No one except Cheryl.

"We could get arrested for this. What if the Prague police are waiting for us when we get off the tram? I've read that in some cities you can be arrested for riding public transportation without paying." She fretted and worried for the entire ride. When we pulled into the stop, we jumped from the train fully expecting to be put into handcuffs and hustled off to a Czechoslovakian prison, never to be heard from again.

All we encountered were crowds – masses of people moving as one unit through the sites of Prague. From Old Town to Prague Castle to The Church of Our Lady Before Tyn to the Jewish Quarter; we mooed along with the herd. By the time we reached Charles Bridge, found a small hole in the wall of people and ran to the nearest pub for cover.

"I can't stand it," Cheryl cried. "There are so many people here. I'm over cites!"

Not a big fan of crowds myself, I was happy we'd found the Pilsner Pub to duck into.

"When did it happen?" I asked as we sipped a beer to calm our nerves.

"Sometime during Switzerland and Austria, I suppose. Spending time enjoying the outdoors became more appealing than 'seeing the sights'."

I was in full agreement. Whether it was not feeling well or the fact we'd been traveling for twelve weeks solid; I was ready for something familiar. I'd taken so many pictures I prayed I'd remember what monument went with which city. We'd slept in so many unfamiliar beds – coils poking through, tiny pillows that crinkled when you mashed them, or those harder than sleeping on a slab of cement – a comfortable bed seemed a distant memory.

So we decided to throw away the tourist map and regain a few strands of our sanity. We walked to the mall. We gawked at the brightly lit neon and we savored the taste of fresh popcorn while we watched the comedy Ratatouille in English at the theatre. We ate dinner at the mall and laughed about the movie. After twelve weeks, even the previews were funny. Czech Goulash with dumplings might not be your typical American mall fare, but I enjoyed every bite.

All around us, conversations were non-stop European football. Soccer mania was in full force. The World Cup games were going on and everyone seemed excited about their chances.

We head back to our hostel for our last night in Prague and climb the stairs to strains of *La Bamba* being sung in a language we only guess to be Czech. Other instruments are being tuned for backup.

"It's going to be a long night," I sighed and turned out the light in our little room at the Prague Pillow in Czechoslovakia.

18

"If you reject the food, ignore the customs, fear the religion and avoid the people, you might better stay at home."

- James A. Michener

Regensburg, Germany

"Can you teach me the toast again?" I ask as we sit in the Biergarten outside of our hotel in Regensburg.

"Okay. It's Eins, Zwei, Drei, and Prost! One, Two, Three, and Cheers!" Cheryl uses her own stein of dunkel to accentuate each syllable. "I knew all those years of German in high school would come in handy," she laughed.

We still had a day before Oktoberfest began, but I didn't want to take any chances on not toasting properly. Our lessons for the festival had already included the proper name for the beer – a Mass served in a one liter Krug. We were told some of the experienced servers can carry up to ten Krugs at once. Wow! I was so excited about being at a party where they'd be serving over six million liters of beer.

"We can't be too disappointed," Cheryl explained. "Everyone has told us that without early reservations, they'll be no way we'll get inside the beer tents. And without a seat, you can't buy beer inside. Even the hikers from Munich we met in Bad Gastein said the same thing. And every time I've tried to get tickets, I was told they were all sold out."

"It's all right. You've been trying to get us tickets since July. We'll enjoy just being there and, if by some miracle we're able to get in, it'll be a bonus." I wasn't worrying that far ahead yet. I was still excited about us finding the hotel where we were staying the next three nights.

Because Oktoberfest was starting up, all of the hotels within a hundred kilometer radius of Munich were full. We spent an hour at the Tourist Center in the adorable picture-book town of Regensburg finding this out.

"There has been one cancellation a few minutes ago," the clerk explained in patient English. "The hotel is hell. Would you like me to book it for you?"

I looked at Cheryl and shrugged. We'd probably stayed in worse places and if it was the only hotel available, it beat sleeping in the car – hell or not.

Cheryl chuckled as the clerk gave us a slip of paper with the directions and our reservation. "The Hotel is Held, with a D. Not Hell. We don't have to sleep in Hotel Hell tonight."

Hotel Held was wonderful. "They have those great smelling soaps and lotions in the bathroom!" I ran out to show Cheryl the stash of stuff. "And even a nail file and sewing kit. This place is fantastic!"

"Better not get too used to that. In a couple of weeks, we'll be living in the Mexican jungle. From the way they describe it, conditions are pretty primitive. Bucket showers and sleeping in huts with mosquito nets. No good-smelling lotions in your bathroom every day."

"Uh-huh, I'm sure it won't be that bad." I refused to let Cheryl's reality impose on my ability to completely hide my head in the sand. If I didn't think about it, it wasn't yet the truth. "And did you notice the hotel has its own Biergarten outside?"

Cheryl just gave her best enigmatic smile. "You're right. Mexico is still a while off. Today it's a perfect fall day, let's go outside and have a beer to celebrate."

While enjoying a couple of their house specials – Brauerei Kneitinger Regensburg – the afternoon chill whetted our appetites.

"Did you notice the restaurant when we checked in?" Cheryl asked.

"I did. I also read their daily specials. A rahmschnitzel, served with a cream sauce, a jagerschnitzel with mushrooms and sour cream, and the obligatory Wiener schnitzel," I sighed heavily. "When we first came to this part of the world, I loved schnitzel. But we've had it for almost every meal. I would give anything for something familiar to eat. Something I can recognize."

"Something not schnitzel," Cheryl agreed. "Let's drive around and see what we can find. Worse case, we can always come back here and eat schnitzel again."

Driving thorough the German countryside was cathartic. Fields of freshly plowed potatoes quickly led to a portion of the German Autobahn. There we took full advantage of the lack of a speed limit. Windows down, enjoying the air blowing through the car, I almost missed it. A blur of blue and it was gone. Once my mind caught up with what my eyes were seeing, I almost screamed. "Back there! Let's go back there! We can eat dinner there!"

"Where?" Cheryl asked, slowing down. "I didn't see any restaurants back there. Just an industrial area."

"Yes. It's industrial, but did you see what was there? Did you see it?" I pointed to the next exit to get us turned around.

"I'm afraid to ask, but what are you talking about?"

"It's an IKEA! Here in Germany! We can eat there. I love their Swedish meatballs and the food is cheap!" I chattered excitedly, already imagining the taste of boysenberry jam with my meatballs.

"You're kidding, right? You want to eat dinner at an IKEA. In Germany?"

"Absolutely! I'll bet they don't serve schnitzel there, either."

In case anyone needs to know – no schnitzel of any kind is served at German IKEAs. However, the Swedish meatballs are wonderful and the German beers on tap make a nice change from smoky Biergartens. Just ignore the sofas and pillow cases on the way in.

On the way back to the hotel, Cheryl extracted a promise. "You know we can't tell anyone we ate dinner at an IKEA, don't you? It's embarrassing. Promise me you won't tell a soul."

My tummy full from familiar fare, I promised not to speak a word of it. Writing it, now that's another matter entirely.

Later that evening, we sat outside to enjoy the fresh air and gloriously full moon. The Biergarten was full as we planned our trip into Munchen the next day by train. A delicate lady holding a dachshund in her lap smiled our way as we chattered about the upcoming festivities.

"This article says there will be five hundred thousand roasted chickens, fifty thousand pork knuckles, and one hundred whole oxen cooked to feed everyone," Cheryl read from the English backpacker's magazine she'd found.

"What a pork knuckle?" I asked.

"Not sure, but we'll try to skip those. I'm sure with that much food, something will strike us."

"And why do they call it Oktoberfest, when it's the last two weeks of September?"

"Not sure about that either, but it does run into the month October. Maybe it sounded better than Septemberfest? I wouldn't worry about it too much."

I wasn't worried. I was excited. "What else does it say?"

"There is a Bavarian dictionary for newcomers. Words to help you navigate Oktoberfest. Like aufmandeln, a verb. Means to make yourself bigger, especially when you're trying to save someone a seat in the beer tents. Or fetznrausch, a noun. It means totally and hugely drunk.Oh, and this is good. A popular activity at Oktoberfest is fingahackln. When two men hook their middle fingers and try to pull one another over the table."

"Oh, this is going to be so much fun!" I clapped my hands in glee. I couldn't wait for tomorrow to come.

Munich, Germany

We found a Park and Ride at a soccer arena (Frottmanning) just a few kilometers outside of Regensburg and thirteen short stops later arrived at Goetheplatz in Munchen. It was easy enough to find where to go from there – we just followed everyone dressed in traditional Bavarian costumes of lederhosen and dirndls. From tiny infants in felt to cane-wielding Grandpas in soft leather, it seemed the entire population had pulled out their best finery for opening day of Oktoberfest.

"The fitted bodice of one of those dresses would look great on you," I observed to Cheryl, "but for me it would be a waste of elastic."

The streets were filled with happy people and we were still blocks from the festival. Winding down side alleys and peeking in gardens, we quickly found ourselves front and center of the celebration Germans are known for.

What a party! My first impression was we'd stumbled on the German equivalent of a state fair; with carousels and pony rides, games and concessions, and long lines at the self-explanatory pissoir.

Wonder of all wonders – there was no cover charge to come in! All of this fun and excitement for free. A parade of Oompah-Pah bands marched by as we arrived and we followed their line in through the gates.

"Where are the tents?" I asked after we'd made one cursory round through the fair. "I don't see any tents."

Worry creased Cheryl's brow as she looked around. "The paper said there were fourteen main tents and some small ones. Friends from work said not to miss the Hippodrome or the Schottenhamel tent. But I don't see any tents, either."

Once again, an Oompah-Pah band saved the day. While we were standing outside the huge array of buildings, trying to locate the tents, the band marched by.

"Let's follow them," Cheryl suggested. "They are probably going to one of the tents." Trailing just behind the horse-drawn cart, we chased the band into a cavernous structure filled with people.

"It's the Lowenbrau House," I shouted reverently, because whispering would have been useless. Booming voices of intoxicated singers rang around us only somewhat in tune with the band we'd befriended. We had found the tents!

From the horror stories we'd been told of people being forcibly removed without reservations or tickets, we tiptoed around the fringes of the enormous place enjoying the music and spectacle from afar. After fifteen minutes or so, we noticed people simply walking in and sitting down. They didn't show a ticket to anyone.

"Cheryl, they're ordering beer! I don't think we need a ticket," I pointed toward an empty spot. "Should we try it?"

Knowing Cheryl to be much braver, I wanted her to be the one forcibly removed if it came down to that. Together, but with Cheryl far in front, we inched forward to a table with two just-vacated seats.

"Is it okay if we sit here?" she asked hesitantly.

"Of course!" came the answer from around the table. We sat down with huge grins and within minutes had met a couple from Washington State and two German men with their four small sons. It was important to know everyone at the table because one of the customs when toasting at Oktoberfest is to always toast everyone at the table, look them in the eye as you clink glasses, and all drink together.

And the glasses were huge! Full, it took both my hands to lift it up and stuff my head inside. The German frauliens delivering the beer didn't disappoint – ours carried nine Krugs from the bar to the table with barely a wince. These ladies were expert servers; managing to sidestep singing, stumbling revelers while balancing massive plates of chicken, sausages, and soup.

Every ten minutes or so, the band would crank up into a song. This was a signal for everyone to stop their conversation, jump up on the table or stand on their bench, join in the song and sway of that particular melody, then methodically toast everyone at the table. All day and all night. It was no wonder the line was so long at the pissoir.

We learned that unlike what we'd heard, it *was* possible to walk into the tents without a reservation. Evenings were harder and some of the more popular tents did have standing room only, but we managed to hit almost every one during our two days at the festival.

"What's your favorite so far?" I asked while loading my mouth with drop-off-the-bone spare ribs. "These are so delicious. Tomato and red pepper, yum!"

"Probably the beef and potato dumpling at the Haufbrau House," she said, finishing off an odd looking sausage on her plate. "The Fisher House was just too fishy smelling with all of those halibut roasting outside. The Hippodrome was fun with all of the streamers and flowers, but it was so smoky and hot."

For two days, we made the rounds, sampling it all. "The pretzels here in Germany put those back in the States to shame. They're enormous – salty and sweet all at once and make you beg for more beer," I noted.

"I think that's the idea," Cheryl laughed.

Venturing outside the tent du jour for some welcome fresh air, we were overwhelmed by the magnitude of delights available. There were gingerbread hearts, candy apples, ice cream, candied fruit, and nuts coated with melted sugar and cinnamon. Every type of sausage imaginable and odd fish sandwiches of herring, cod, and smoked salmon with onions and pickles caught my eye, but Cheryl kept her distance. It was a feast for the senses and the appetite.

"My stomach hurts," I moaned after finishing the last bite of a sticky candy apple.

"Mine, too," Cheryl agreed. "I think it's time we were on our way. We've got a long journey back to Paris. In a week we'll be back home. The trip is almost over."

I nodded sadly. It had been over three months since we'd left – and in some ways it felt like just yesterday.

19

"All travel has its advantages. If the passenger visits better countries, he may learn to improve his own. And if fortune carries him to worse, he may learn to enjoy it."
                               - Samuel Johnson

Epernay, France

"Can we get arrested for this?" I whispered as we ducked behind one of the endless rows of grapevines facing the hotel.

"I don't know, so be careful. The ground is rocky and slippery here." Cheryl ran ahead and disappeared into the rapidly descending twilight. We were alone in a massive vineyard just outside of Epernay. Miles and miles of symmetrical arbors rose up before us in a maze of autumn colors.

"It feels like we're standing in the middle of The Great Pumpkin Patch!" I said, shivering with excitement. "I expect to bump into Linus at any moment."

We were trespassing in this delightful grove of grapes because I wanted a picture while the light was perfect. My fondest desire being to capture the essence of this part of France before the chilly rains came again and forced us back inside to watch European football in a smoky brasserie smelling of wet wool and goulash.

We'd found a familiar Campanile hotel meeting our now basic criteria for a place to sleep – a good price and easy to locate on the map. The last few cold, rainy days on the road had us longing for comfort food and their restaurant's beefsteak with buttery tagliatelle noodles soothed every time.

Checking in late afternoon, the first thing I noticed was the vineyard surrounding the hotel. In fact, the hotel was only a tiny freckle on the face of this well-groomed hill of Epernay grapes.

"Look! Beautiful grapes!" I shouted, jumping from the car at as close to a sprint as I could muster after being in the car all day. "There must be millions of them!"

Tugging at camera bags in the back seat and tipping over precariously perched sacks of groceries, I set off to tromp through the vineyard like a kid, cameras banging behind me.

With a slightly sour smell enveloping us from all sides, we assumed those grapes left on the vine were the last of the season. "Let's taste one," I suggested.

"What is with you and eating things from the road?" Cheryl asked in horror. "You'll pick berries, not even knowing what they are, and eat them. Anything from the side of the road is fair game."

"These aren't from the road. They're safe in a vineyard. Quit worrying. We can't be sure the sign out front specifically says, No Trespassing. It's in French. Go ahead, be daring, try one!"

Looking furtively over the top of the vine we were ducked behind, we each picked a perfect specimen and popped it into our mouths.

"Oh, that really tastes…nasty!" I tried to swallow as my throat closed against the sour bite.

Cheryl's face froze into a powerful pucker. "It's horrible!" she sputtered when she was able to form words again.

"Hopefully, these aren't the grapes used to make Dom Perignon," I moaned. Epernay was on our list to visit specifically because in my mind's eye I could see the label of a coveted bottle of Dom Perignon champagne listing its origins as Epernay, France. Any place with its name on the bottle of Dom must be a special place.

Over dinner, we perused the list of local attractions. "They have an Avenue of Champagne here," I whispered in awe. Imagining gilded streets lined with sparkling flutes glittering in the sunshine, this visit was put front and center for our next day to-do list.

We awoke to a torrential downpour and even cooler temperatures than the day before. Bundled in most of our wardrobe, we slogged toward the downtown area of Epernay.

"At least you were able to get some great pictures of the grapes yesterday," Cheryl added hopefully.

I glared in her direction as I tripped into yet another puddle at the Church of Notre Dame parking lot. The gloominess of the day only heightened my feeling that the gargoyles were watching our every move.

"Normally you love gargoyles," Cheryl observed. "What is it about these you don't like?"

"I'm not sure. These are creepy." I walked over to the bank of stained glass windows, learning this depiction of the life of the Virgin Mary had been brought to Epernay in the sixteenth century. So beautiful, yet I couldn't shake the chill.

"Did you know this church stands on the original site of an Ursuline convent?" Cheryl read from the flyer she'd picked up. "And the town of Epernay has been destroyed, ransacked, and burnt over twenty-five times since it was founded? Amazing!"

I began to feel comfortable again when we shut out the rain and cold in exchange for dry and warmth of a local pizzeria. Bright smells of garlic and lasagna pushed away the grayness of the day for a while, even though the wind blustered just outside the rattling front door.

"Our champagne tour doesn't start until two," Cheryl said. "What would you like to do until then?"

With choices of getting wet or wetter, cold or colder; I opted for two of my favorite things. "Let's just stay here. Order dessert and another carafe of wine."

Cheryl agreed readily.

At one-thirty we made our grand entrance. A reflection of fresh-cut flowers gleamed from the marble floor. Gigantic mirrors reflected the opulence of the Moët & Chandon residence at Number Twenty Avenue of Champagne. Jazz music played while Cheryl enjoyed an international newspaper for the first time in weeks. I was reading the tasting menu in anticipation of the Champagne we'd sample after our tour.

"There he is! There he is!" I pointed excitedly when we'd arrived.

"Who? Who do you see?"

"It's Dom. See? Dom of Dom Perignon!" I could die happy now. I'd spotted the statue of the Benedictine monk who lived 1638 until 1715 and was credited with discovering how to produce champagne using the Méthode Champenoise. "He would call to the other monks, 'Come quickly, I am drinking the stars!'"

"Then let's go inside and drink the stars, too!" Cheryl said.

Before we could sip, we first had the tour. Twenty-five meters below the ground exist the miles of cellars – home to millions of bottles of Champagne! In the damp, dark, sweetly-scented cellar, we learned there are several stages of fermentation until the Champagne is ready to be sold.

"Wow!" I whispered as our tour guide explained a sugar and yeast mixture called Liqueur de Tirage is added to the wine, causing carbon dioxide bubbles to form. "That's what tickles our nose," I added before Cheryl shushed me.

She was trying to listen as the guide gave details of how the yeast sediment is removed from the bottles. "Wine bottles are placed in these racks at a forty-five degree angle. Every few days, a person highly experienced in Riddling, comes and gives the bottle a shake and a small turn."

"I wonder if The Riddler ever gets Carpal Tunnel Syndrome?" I murmured in a soft voice. Evidently, it wasn't soft enough, because this time I got an angry look from both the tour guide and Cheryl. Sheepishly, I promised to be quiet while he finished the story.

"After six to eight weeks, the bottle angle is increased and all the sediment collects in the neck of the bottle. This neck is frozen, the bottle is opened, and out pops the block of wine sediment. A mixture of sugar and blended wine is added to replace what was lost from freezing and the bottle is given is final cork."

I was amazed. Not only at how the Champagne was made, but also at how far the cellars extended underground. "Could you imagine getting lost down here? Miles and miles of dusty bottles, some dating back to Napoleon's time. What a story that would make," I sighed wistfully. From that moment until we were safely on our way to Paris, Cheryl refused to let me out of her sight.

Paris, France

What do you do on the last full day in Europe? Why, visit Paris again, of course!

It's been thirteen and a half weeks traveling. Twelve countries. Wondrous sights. Many new words and new friends. And one last trip to the Hard Rock Café Paris – this time to pick up a birthday present for Cheryl's sister-in-law.

It was three Metro stops from our airport hotel and she was a trooper, only checking behind us every few minutes to be sure we weren't being singled out again. Having our wallets stolen at this stage of the trip might have pushed us over the edge.

"My mind is going in a million directions," I complained. "Have we missed anything? Is everything set for Mexico in six days? Do we have all the required shots for Africa in January? What are we going to eat first when we get back home?"

"Let's go to the Louvre," Cheryl suggested. "We won't have time to worry about all the details we can't do anything about now anyway. We'll spend the afternoon there."

Her idea made me very happy. I'd only been to the famous museum once before on a whirlwind Paris trip many years before with my mother. On that trip, the museum had been about to close and all I remember was running through hallways, following signs to be able to say I'd seen the Mona Lisa. This time we could enjoy her at leisure.

A sign announcing *The Da Vinci Code Tour* pulled us into the Denon Wing. Ten euros later we were holding cassette machines around our necks and jogging around the museum with voices of the characters in our ears.

"Stop here and pull back the drapes. Here you'll see the spot where....." the narrator explained.

"This is so much fun," Cheryl said. "It brings the Louvre to life."

Seeing Leonardo Da Vinci's masterpieces in person was a treat after spending so much time at the places where he'd been born and died. "He finished this painting in the rose garden where we had a glass of wine," I mused as we waited our turn for a look at the diminutive Mona Lisa.

"I didn't realize she was so small," Cheryl noted. The size of the painting seemed to be the general discussion of everyone where we were standing.

By late afternoon we'd worn our feet weary. We headed out to the Tuileries Gardens and sat down for a while to savor a brief spot of sunshine and watch the people pass. When the Seine beckoned, we listened and found a perfect sidewalk café to order a pinchet of vin rouge and a jambon de pays (country ham on warm toast). The bouquinistes were busy packing up their stalls for the night and flickers of lamplight began to appear on the ponts. Saying goodbye to Paris properly – for now – we proceeded to the Metro station and our hotel. It would be an early flight back home.

20

"No one realizes how beautiful it is to travel until he comes home and rests his head on his old, familiar pillow."

- Lin Yutang

Paris, France to Tampa, Florida

"Do you realize we've been on the road since June and it's now October? A whole summer has passed," I mused as we tossed our bags on the scale to be weighed at Charles de Gaulle airport.

Only twenty-five pounds this time. We'd lightened our load significantly by mailing home a box of souvenirs and pamphlets accumulated along the way. Did I really need to keep a crumpled map of Dublin? Or was the pile of newspapers from Spain a necessity when I couldn't read them anyway? Free the clutter and your load will be lighter – my new motto. Whatever.

In eight hours and forty-five minutes we'd be landing in the United States. Home. Why did it feel so strange? This morning we'd updated our Travelpod blog for the last time on this trip. Read e-mails from home concerning lives we'd left behind. A friend is pregnant with twins! Cheryl's hairdresser saw her pictures on-line and offered to "fix" her for free. My cats were doing well and adjusting to their new home in New Orleans. Our lives had been a moving walkway the past few months and now it was time to stand on familiar ground for a short while.

Close friends offered to take us in for the five days between Europe and the ten week Mexican volunteer expedition. Just enough time to re-pack all of our gear again – this time with an emphasis on SCUBA gear and sunscreen rather than dress clothes for a possible audience with the Pope.

Staying with friends meant sleeping in a comfortable bed under the roof of people we loved, eating foods we could recognize and pronounce, and most importantly, doing all of our laundry.

Because we flew in late the night before, Sandy and Steve left us to our own devices for the morning. "Help yourself," Sandy said on her way out to work. "Use the washer and dryer and anything you need in the laundry room."

We were in business. Priscilla, the purple octopus, was freed from the confines of the pack where she'd been stuffed. Wadded and wrinkled clothes were yanked out of backpacks, sorted, and piled up on the floor.

Cheryl disappeared for a few minutes, then announced, "My clothes are in the washer, so when you're ready you can add yours and turn it on."

I looked up a bit sleepily while nursing a huge cup of coffee, but did manage a nod and tried to engage my brain toward the task at hand. I gave myself time to let the caffeine kick in a little, then grabbed an armload of dirties and headed toward the laundry room.

Americans really have it all together when it comes to cleaning clothes. Things I had taken for granted while we traveled, but never would again: bright, shiny machines with large capacities, settings for different sized loads, even an ability for the machine to determine exactly how long it takes to dry a particular load of clothes. Wow! Amazing!

And not to mention the vast array of choices for soaping, fluffing, and infusing our garments with delicious smells from wash through the drying cycle. I looked over the shelves of Sandy's laundry room like a child in an ice cream shop.

I made my choices – Mountain Fresh detergent, Seaside Summer fabric softener, and reverently folder two Lavender Lullaby dryer sheets for when the load was done. All guaranteed to make me smell my best since I'd left the States thirteen weeks before. I was an aromatherapy melting pot waiting to happen.

Opening the door to the washer with my brain still not engaged, it wasn't until I was about to throw my stuff in that I realized the machine was empty.

"Cheryl, didn't you say you'd put in your laundry already?" I shouted back toward the last direction I'd seen her.

"Yes, it's in there. You just need to add the soap and turn it on."

This time I stuck my whole head inside. Nada. It was too early for practical jokes and I knew she hadn't had her coffee yet, so this mystery I had to figure out on my own. My clues were an empty laundry basket and an empty washing machine. There was only one other place they could be.

Beside the washer sat its identical twin – a brand new dryer, ready and waiting to plump up our clothes and give them back cuddly warm. Yep, that's where they were. When I told her about it later, she grinned. "Oops, it's been so long since I've used one of those, I guess I forgot the difference between a washer and dryer. Are you sure you're ready to travel with me again? To Mexico? And then to South Africa?"

"Hey, this is just the beginning," I said. "We're going around the world! There are so many things to see and books to write. People need to know it's possible to live a dream like this. We're living proof, even if we can't wash our own clothes."

"The next part of the journey won't be as comfortable as Europe," Cheryl explained. "In Mexico, we'll be living in the jungle with only minimal niceties – no running water, refrigeration, or air conditioning. Primitive. In South Africa, it's strictly camping in the bush. Up close and personal with nature. Think you'll be up for that?"

"Hey, we'll be doing something good by volunteering. We're not tourists anymore, we're travelers," I said smugly, tossing a wine opener into the pile of essential gear. "And anyway, how hard can it be?"

About The Travelers

Cheryl MacDonald – Planner and Mistress of the Checklist for every facet of this journey.

Leaving a Corporate Director position at a Fortune 500 company and traveling the world wasn't originally on Cheryl's carefully typed list of "to-do's". But when it became a choice of her health over her career, she wisely chose to take the road less traveled. "I'd never left the country before. I always said 'maybe someday' I'll go. But there is an amazing world to discover. I'm glad I didn't wait!"

Cheryl left a sixteen year career to travel the world and make a difference doing it. She has spoken in motivational clinics and executive development programs for Women Unlimited and Medco Health Services. At the age of forty, she decided to complete her SCUBA Rescue Diver and Dive Master certifications

Favorite Travel Quote: *The wise man travels to discover himself."*
~ **James Russell Lowell**

Lisa Chavis – Dreamer and Scribe.

All too ready to pack up and go on an adventure, Lisa's rude awakening came when the last of her possessions were sold and she faced bare rooms for the first time. "I knew my life had changed forever when I didn't have a home or things to come back to anymore. But the whole world was out there in front of me and I couldn't wait to go out and see it!"

Lisa's previous publishing credits include *Ask Your Pharmacist – A Leading Pharmacist Answers Your Most Frequently Asked Questions* (St. Martin's Press) and *The Family Pharmacist* (Perigee). Lisa Chavis has media experience as a featured guest on CNN's Weekend House Call, as well as a National Radio Tour. She has been quoted as an expert in *Parade* magazine, *Fitness*, and *Ladies Home Journal*.

Favorite Travel Quote: *"Not all those who wander are lost."* ~ **J.R.R. Tolkien**

Priscilla – Purple Octopus and Photograph Model.

While she *is* quiet by nature, she never complained the entire trip. No matter how many times she was stuffed in a backpack or remained behind in the hostel while we were out and about exploring.

Favorite Travel Quote: *"We all live in a Yellow Submarine."* ~ **The Beatles**

What Boundaries? Live Your Dream!
Travel Blog can be found at www.WhatBoundaries.com.
You can also follow Lisa and Cheryl on
Twitter **@what_boundaries** and on **Facebook**.

Questions And Answers

We're often asked questions about this *What Boundaries? Live Your Dream!* adventure and thought it might be fun to answer a few for you here.

- **Why the use of travel quotations to begin each chapter?**
    - With each facet of our journey, we relied on inspiration from many different sources. Repeating a favorite travel mantra over and over often kept us from bursting into tears or running screaming down the street when things didn't go as planned.
- **What gave you the courage to sell your possessions and take off to travel the world?**
    - Tequila.
- **Is traveling with a good friend something you would recommend for others?**
    - Getting sick of each other was something we worried about at great length before the trip. Once we were traveling, however, we worried about getting lost, finding a place to eat, whether the beds were clean, and how much longer we'd be lugging the heavy backpack. Having a friend around during all this was a nice bonus.
- **What was the most exciting place you visited on this trip?**
    - *Cheryl*: Bunol, Spain for La Tomatina. I've never experienced an energy like we felt on those streets in the crush of bodies and a real tomato tossing fight!
    - *Lisa*: For me, it was Paris. As a self-described Ernest Hemingway stalker, this was as close to his ghost as I could imagine. The sights, smells, and spirits of Paris are unlike those anywhere else in the world.
- **What was the funniest event you two experienced?**
    - *Cheryl*: Watching Lisa get attacked by wild horses in Austria. She was yelling for help and I couldn't stop laughing. A herd of hungry horses against one apple and one short traveler aren't the best odds.

- - *Lisa*: In hindsight, it had to be getting tangled in the moving airport walkway in Nice and stranding an entire group of German tourists behind me. Sorry guys!
- **What was the most difficult part of the journey?**
  - The enormous albatross called a backpack that kept following us!
- **What was the most rewarding part?**
  - The friends we made (and continue to make) along the way.
- **Would you do it again?**
  - Absolutely! Only the next time we travel, it will be with a carry-on and a Kindle.
- **Are you finished traveling for a while?**
  - After Europe, we're scheduled for ten weeks in Mexico for coral reef conservation and ten weeks in S. Africa to volunteer on a game reserve. Then Egypt, Jordan, Malaysia, Thailand, China, Hong Kong, and Indonesia for touring and to hone our diving skills. Afterwards, we're planning to be back in US to discover Hawaii and Alaska, and then it's going to be a road trip to visit and write about animal rescue centers across the States. So, to answer the question – no, not yet. ;-)

www.ingramcontent.com/pod-product-compliance
Lightning Source LLC
LaVergne TN
LVHW041618070426
835507LV00008B/317